Ageless Counsel for Modern Life:

Profound Commentaries on the I Ching
By an Achieved Taoist Master

Taoist Master
NI, HUA-CHING

The Shrine of the Eternal Breath of Tao
College of Tao & Traditional Chinese Healing
LOS ANGELES

The Shrine of the Eternal Breath of Tao,
Malibu, California 90265

College of Tao and Traditional Chinese Healing
1314 Second Street #A
Santa Monica, California 90401

Library of Congress Cataloging-in-Publication Data

Ni, Hua-Ching.
    Ageless counsel for modern life : profound commentaries on the
I Ching by an achieved taoist master / Ni, Hua-Ching.
            p.   cm.
    ISBN 0-937064-50-5 : $15.95
    1. I ching.   I. Title
PL2464.Z6N5   1991   91-53212
299'.51282--dc20   CIP

This book is dedicated to those who
concentrate themselves in their broad and
balanced spiritual development, which arms
them with spiritual versatility and tenacity.

To female readers,

According to Taoist teaching, male and female are equally important in the natural sphere. This is seen in the diagram of Tai Chi. Thus, discrimination is not practiced in our tradition. All my work is dedicated to both genders of human people.

Wherever possible, constructions using masculine pronouns to represent both sexes are avoided; where they occur, we ask your tolerance and spiritual understanding. We hope that you will take the essence of my teaching and overlook the superficiality of language. Gender discrimination is inherent in English; ancient Chinese pronouns do not have differences of gender. I wish for all of your achievement above the level of language or gender.

Thank you, H. C. Ni

Warning - Disclaimer

This book is intended to present information and techniques that have been in use throughout the orient for many years. The information offered is to the author's best knowledge and experience and is to be used by the reader(s) at their own discretion. This information and practices utilize a natural system within the body, however, there are no claims for effectiveness.

Because of the sophisticated nature of the information contained within this book, it is recommended that the reader of this book also study the author's other books for further knowledge about a healthy lifestyle and energy conducting exercises.

People's lives have different conditions. People's growth has different stages. Because the background of people's development cannot be unified, no rigid or stiff practice is given that can be applied universally. Thus, it must be through the discernment of the reader that the practices are selected. The adoption and application of the material offered in this book must be your own responsibility.

The author and publisher of this book are not responsible in any manner whatsoever for any injury which may occur through following the instructions in this book.

Contents

Prelude

"Tao is the destination of all religions, while it leaves behind all religions just like the clothing of different seasons and different places. Tao is the goal of serious science, but it leaves behind all sciences as a partial and temporal description of the Integral Truth.

"The teaching of Tao includes all religious subjects, yet it is not on the same level as religions. Its breadth and depth go far beyond the limits of religion. The teaching of Tao serves people's lives like religions do, yet it transcends all religions and contains the essence of all religions.

"The teaching of Tao is not like any of the sciences. It is above the level of any single subject of science.

"The teaching of Tao is the master teaching of all. However, it does not mean the teaching relies on a master. It means the teaching of Tao is like a master key which can unlock all doors leading to the Integral Truth. It teaches or shows the truth directly. It does not stay on the emotional surface of life or remain at the level of thought or belief. Neither does it stay on the intellectual level of life, maintaining skepticism and searching endlessly. The teaching of Tao presents the core of the subtle truth and helps you to reach it yourself.

Preface

The *Book of Changes* is also known as the *I Ching* (pronounced ee ching.) The *I Ching* is the broad and important foundation of the learning of Tao. Combined with the classic Taoist teachings, enlightenment, gentle physical movement and esoteric practice and leaving aside specific training such as Taoist medicine, etc., it weighs as one fifth of the learning of Tao. It offers wide and deep benefits to all aspects of a person's life as well as to human society. In this preface I hope to deepen your understanding of the *I Ching* by comparing some significant differences present in the Taoist and Confucian interpretation.

I arrived in the United States in 1977. At the request of my students, I held a set of classes to teach the *I Ching* or *Book of Changes*. At this time, I also had the opportunity to examine the widely recognized Wilhelm translation with the introduction by Carl Jung. I studied his rendition and found that he did a good job and gave a very scholarly translation. I noticed that his Chinese *I Ching* teacher was a Confucian scholar. Coincidentally, I had been in southern China at the time Wilhelm was there learning from Lao Nai-hsuan in northern China. I found the stiffness of the Confucian doctrines evidenced throughout his version.

The class took quite a long time to teach. I did not tape record the classes at the beginning because my English at that time was still very poor. I did make tapes of some of the last classes, which were only a few words among much noise. Yet, these tapes served to stimulate my memory when I later put the hexagrams into written form. When I taught a second series of classes on the *I Ching*, I tape recorded and transcribed all the lectures with the help of the students who were in the classes. The quality of the tapes was not much better, but I was able to use them to write a new version of the *I Ching*. So from this process, in 1983, I published the *Book of Changes and the Unchanging Truth*. It received very good response from a large group of readers and people interested in making use of the *I Ching* in their lives. Through my cultivation of this process, I grew able to understand and articulate clearly the essence of the *I Ching* from a Taoist point of view. I can also discuss how it differs in principle from a Confucian viewpoint. The next segment of this preface will directly address those differences.

The study of the *I Ching* has two main schools: Confucianist and Taoist. What I present is from my own spiritual training. Here, I would like to give you some understanding about the difference between the Confucian school and the Taoist school of the study of the *I Ching*.

The Confucian school gives rigid explanations that stress the meaning of the fixed positions of different lines. For example, they made yang to be superior and yin as inferior. Superior is also male, Heaven, king or emperor, husband, father, etc. Yin or inferior is also female, earth, minister and people, wife, mother, etc. Those categories are represented as the unchangeable reality of natural position. Confucius used the *I Ching* to support his special theory of the patriarchal or father-centered society. For example, the use of the term "superior man" meant an aristocrat to Confucius and those who study him. Students of Tao would rather consider a "superior person" to be a spiritually developed person of whatever social position or gender.

The Taoist study of the *I Ching* began much earlier than Confucius. The achieved ones in Tao do not accept all that Confucius structured as his idea of an orderly world and orderly society. My book presents the understanding of true Taoism, in which no fixed or rigid meaning nor application of hexagrams and lines can be held as ultimate truth.

As we know, in ancient times, there were three versions of the *I Ching*. The first one is the original *I Ching* developed by Fu Shi. It was very simple; it had diagrams and drawings but no written language. In it, the receptive earth (yin) energy was given before the creative sky (yang) energy. This follows the Taoist belief that the spiritual nature of the universe is feminine. The second version is by Shen Nung (reign 3218-3078 B.C.). It was written during the start of agricultural development. Shen Nung added explanations or elucidations to describe what the hexagrams meant. The first version by Fu Shi remained in all versions of the *Book of Changes*, because it was only the hexagrams. The second version by Shen Nung no longer exists.

The third version was by King Wen (active time around 1191-1120 B.C.) and his son, Duke Jou (active time around 1104 B.C.). Duke Jou made his elucidation of the *I Ching* fit his idea of the new social establishment, or rather the way he wanted the social establishment to be. He reordered the hexagrams to put Chyan, yang energy, before K'un, yin energy, and put different elucidations than the ones done by Shen Nung. Confucius (551-479 B.C.) kept the version restructured by Duke Jou, with the intention of fully establishing a culturally father-centered society. It became the existing version of the *I Ching*. It is different from the earlier versions which were developed when the world was more natural; when motherly loving energy was more recognized and valued than the masculine conquering force which grew to be the image of the leaders of later society.

Basically, in the *I Ching* of King Wen and Duke Jou or Confucius - especially Confucius - Heaven or God was the ruling power of nature. But in the Taoist view, although human nature needs to accord with the yin nature of earth, the yin nature of earth also needs to accord with the yang nature of Heaven. The yang nature of Heaven needs to accord with the nature of Tao (the subtle universal law), which is above the discrimination of yin and yang.

The *Book of Changes* teaches the energetic nature of change. For positive change to occur, appropriateness and properness must be reached. Because that is different from situation to situation, no rigid standard can be given. The subtle truth, which is what guides correct behavior, is not predisposed to absolute interpretation. The subtle truth requires flexibility, adjustability and changeability.

For example, the natural base of a hexagram is:

Upper or External	▬▬ ▬▬	yin
	▬▬▬▬▬	yang
	▬▬ ▬▬	yin
Lower or internal	▬▬▬▬▬	yang
	▬▬ ▬▬	yin
	▬▬▬▬▬	yang

We call this a base of a hexagram because it is an ideal situation or a correct situation. It represents a state of normalcy or perfect harmony. It is a natural foundation or base upon which whatever change would happen. Because the foundation is based upon a natural, ever-changing energy formation, it does not support any theory that a king must be obeyed, elders must be listened to, a teacher must always be followed, or men must be superior and women must be inferior, etc. No rigid interpretation of the *I Ching* energies or hexagrams is possible, because the universe itself is a continuous big movement which contains small movement: it is a development. All development occurs to adapt to a new situation.

The meaning of the lines within a hexagram is the basis underlying the positions of the lines. The lines of the hexagram are ordered from the bottom to the top. Yang energy is poised on the odd numbered positions and yin energy is poised on the even numbered positions. This expresses the right energy in the right position. A harmonious or supportive situation is implied in such circumstance. Otherwise, disharmonious or improperness is expressed. The specific meaning still depends on the specific hexagram. Positions of different hexagrams need either strong or gentle energy, a sturdy or soft approach. Yin lines or yang lines should not be interpreted as the position of male or female.

An illustration of this principle is given by hexagram #63, where all lines are in the right position, and #64, where all the lines are in the wrong positions. Both structure different pictures and each line of both hexagrams have different meanings.

To make the story short, the unfilled model of a hexagram is a kind of blank upon which any of the 64 combinations can be made. In all trigrams, the upper trigram represents the outside or a large environment, society, the nation or the world, and the lower trigram represents the inside or a small environment of a family or society. The central line in each trigram (the second and the fifth line) is the leader of that trigram. Typically, the fifth line, the central line of the upper trigram, is also the leader of both trigrams and the hexagram.

The Confucian understanding of the *I Ching* interprets hexagram #63 to rigidly mean that in a situation of normalcy, only men can be leaders of the world or nation and only women can be leaders of society or the family. This is too rigid. A responsible and helpful housewife giving help outside the family or as famous leader is considered by Confucian scholars as the hen trying to do the crowing for the rooster.

The learning of Tao interprets that the fifth, yang position of leadership as big as the world or nation, or as small as any group or family, need to be filled by a person with yang or leader energy, who has good health, a balanced personality and strong intelligence. This does not mean that the leader must be a man, but that the energy must be the appropriate yang or leader energy no matter whether man or woman. The second yin line needs to be someone manifesting yin energy. It could be a woman, but it also could be a man, such as in a family and other harmonious occasions. There are many women with yang energy and many men with yin energy. All can find proper life expression with the different energy they possess. It is not their sex origin which brings the differences.

This point is important enough for me to state again in different words. Things or forms cannot be rigidly defined in terms of their form, because various energies move through them, giving them different functions and expressions. For example, a teacher is a person who does not necessarily know everything, nor does he do all the things he knows. On many occasions, a teacher must also be a student, or someone or something else, like an investor, businessman, father, or husband.

Confucius' ideal of a conventional society tends to rigidify or limit things. Thus, any leader (king or emperor) who establishes this type of mentality loses the flexible foundation of governing appropriately and also rigidifies the society which follows his leadership. Religions and cultures were established the same way. This is not the *I Ching* taught by a true teacher of Tao.

There are four parts to my version of the *Book of Changes*, all of which came from the great heritage that existed long before written language developed. In the first part, I discuss the view of the early people with unspoiled mind and their understanding of nature.

In the second part I discuss the hexagrams. Six lines or two trigrams form a hexagram. Each hexagram has a text which explains what that particular hexagram means. They offer special suggestions to help you see where you stand as you face a situation. Usually the hexagram descriptions tell you more than what is already in your conscious mind. Thus, when you throw the coins or stalks, or use the seeds to do a divination, you are usually wishing to obtain access to information about a situation which is in your subconscious mind. The process of divination is basically for the vision of your subconscious mind to be made known to the conscious mind. When you put the two together, conscious and subconscious, a balanced possible direction or solution may be found. However, that is not enough. That only reflects how you project your mind in that moment. Once your mind and attitude changes, or you obtain new information about the situation, then the information from the *I Ching* also changes.

Thinking can be compared to observing your face in a mirror. Just as you can change the expression on your face, you can change your thoughts. However, just as the expression on your face does not always relate precisely to the events that are happening around you, so your mind or thinking may be unrelated to actual external events. Quite often, a situation is fine, but the thoughts are full of subjective worry, concern, vexation, or unrelated disturbance. That unclarity is the reason most people consult the *I Ching*. It is important that an *I Ching* practitioner understand this and train one's mind in order to always find the right answer in the use of the *I Ching*. I am implying that if a person asks a question, and the conscious mind is unclear because of worry, etc., that the hexagram that is thrown will not be the correct one. I am also saying that the subconscious mind will throw a correct hexagram, but the conscious mind will be unable to interpret it accurately. Thus, it is important to calm oneself down and quiet the mind by meditating for a short while, perhaps 20 - 30 minutes, before consulting the oracle. But the meditation also affects the picture of the mind. When it is done in the early morning or at night when there is no energy intrusion or disturbance, then it will be more probable that an accurate result will occur.

The interpretations of the 64 hexagrams can only offer a different way of looking at a situation in question. It kind of gives a specific image or picture to try to help you understand a situation differently.

The third part of the book is at the end. I give some examples of people who achieved lucid vision or clear understanding of the world from using the *I Ching*. They can give you inspiration. They are good examples of *I Ching* practitioners, who with spiritual training, were able to transform and make their lives different from that of all other people in the world.

The fourth part of *The Book of Changes and the Unchanging Truth*, one which my readers think is very useful, is the commentaries placed after each hexagram. In those commentaries, suggestions are given which can be utilized in everyday life, without the need of divination. Many people expressed to me that they were very much helped by using the commentaries as spiritual guidance in everyday life. Many readers requested that the commentaries be printed apart from the big text. They felt it would be helpful for ease in reading and ability to carry along when making a trip or going to work. The commentaries could be read at comfortable intervals. In addition, some publishers contacted us with similar request. So we are responding to your needs. This book is published for your convenience. The commentaries have been slightly revised with improvements. I hope that you find inspiration from them without the need for divination, and that you can use some good attitudes and principles to guide you in your everyday life. I hope these commentaries enrich your life.

Ni, Hua-Ching
July 11, 1991
U.S.A.

Chapter 1

The Primal Chi

What is the universe, and how can the universe be continually alive? It is a big piece of energy; its continuity is the expression of the continual transformation of primal chi as the reality of the universe. Primal chi is the primal energy. On its subtle level, it is the soul of the living universe. It functions as the subtle connection of the universe in the same way that the nervous system functions in the human body. It extends itself primordially as the self-nature of the universe. It then extends itself further as the main spheres of reality, the manifest and the unmanifest.

In the unmanifest sphere, called pre-Heaven, there is nothing describable nor discernible; there is only absolute, undivided oneness. In the manifest sphere of post-Heaven three-dimensional developments are revealed as spirit, matter and life. The diversification of primal chi becomes the multiplicity of individual things and beings.

Although the manifestations of primal chi are many, the reality is one. Expressing the oneness of the universe, it is given the name "Tao." When the primal chi reaches everywhere, it still expresses the oneness of the universe, it is called "Tao." Tao is the flexible and transformable reality of the universe. By its nature, it is given the name "chi."

When primal chi is unexpressed and untransformed as Tao, it is the essence of the universe with inexhaustible potency. When it is expressed as chi, it takes the form of the mother giving birth to her child.

By understanding that all things in the universe are different expressions of chi, one can see why the sages have always said, "All things are one, and the one is all things." Without the outreach and withdrawal, the giving and returning of chi, the transformation of all things would be impossible.

According to Taoist thought, Heaven is not separate from the material sphere as it is in most Western religions. The Taoist Heaven has many energy levels that include all spheres of manifestation. In other words, everything in the universe is a manifestation of Heaven, and everyone is potentially a Heavenly being.

The four great realms of Heaven include: chi as the first, spirit as the second, matter as the third and life as the fourth. The pure and light chi develops into spirits. The impure and heavy chi develops into matter. From the integration of both comes life, thus chi is spirit, chi is matter, and chi is life. Chi is the basic essence of the universe. Nothing that exists can be without it, though it is not everything itself. When regarded as the invisible, untouchable, inaudible, insubstantial substance of the universe, the primal chi is Tao, the path itself. All things manifest or develop from it. In this same way, chi as life can also be differentiated.

A well-trained Kung Fu expert can break stones with his hands as easily as one can cut through a watermelon with a knife. He can demonstrate his truly unusual powers in numerous ways. His performance originates from the chi he has gathered and cultivated.

Some people perform the magical performance of being able to walk on glowing coals in their bare feet. It is chi which enables them to do this. Some psychics can move a chair from one side of a room to the other by either gazing at it or thinking of it. It is chi which makes this possible. Or the woman who gives birth to a dozen children and still looks young and healthy. Again, it is chi which makes this possible. Some Taoists who live in the mountains have outlived several generations of people. It is the cultivation of chi which has made this possible for them.

In an integral or holistic life, the word "chi" has many usages. There is chi in spiritual cultivation, chi in integral, natural medicine, chi in philosophical discussions and chi in everyday use, as in the atmosphere and one's general condition. The usage of the word corresponds to its particular application. Similarly, discovering and understanding chi corresponds to the level of one's personal development.

Taoist cultivation is totally involved with the knowledge and technique of nurturing and managing chi. After thoroughly understanding and mastering the use of chi, one's perception of universal reality deepens, and with it comes the possibility of high spiritual achievement. The summoning of a spirit becomes as sure and trustworthy as extending an invitation to a good friend. Ordinary religions believe that God can do things that are impossible for human beings to accomplish. This is not completely accurate, unless one thoroughly understands that God is chi and, at the same time, spirit. By understanding chi it becomes clear in one's mind that all things are possible by managing chi. What you beseech God to do for you does indeed happen. But what actually makes it happen? It is chi. How does chi make it happen? An individual's personal cultivation creates a certain type or frequency of chi or energy, and there is a responsive answer of the similar frequency from the universe. This is actually not unusual; it happens all the time at the everyday level of life. Special, unusual occurrences or interesting things happening on the spiritual level are usually due to special circumstances or devotion on the part of the individual.

To become "pure chi" is the goal of this immortal tradition. When one's chi becomes purified, one's spirit becomes complete. Then a new immortal is born in the Immortal Realm. Is this not an important and serious matter for everyone?[1]

This chi has many functions. The main ones are as the productivity of the universe. At the same time, it is the creativity of the universe. It is the essence of the universal nature. It is the vitality and resilience of nature. In its first expression, it is the impetus of nature. Thus, it is considered the energy of Chyan or pure, positive yang energy.

---

[1](See the author's work *Tao, the Subtle Universal Law*, for more illustrations of chi.)

Chapter 2

The Balance of Life:
Integrating the Tai Chi

In the previous hexagram, Chyan ☰ , the universal
first nature is discussed. The recognizable trace of the
universal nature can be sensed as the qualities of initiative,
persistence, forwardness, creativeness, productiveness and
positivity. It symbolizes masculinity and fatherhood.

The hexagram K'un ☷ means to accomplish, continue, receive, follow, realize, formalize, shape and stabilize.
It symbolizes femininity or motherhood, and expresses the
self-balancing nature of the universe. Self-balancing means
harmonizing with all beings and things that are brought
forth.

Hands are a good example of how Chyan and K'un
express themselves in the human body. The two types of
energy express the same reality of the one primal energy.
Gentleness is expressed by the soft left hand and strength
is expressed by the strong right hand. Developed people
value the left hand; undeveloped people value the right
hand. Actually, both hands assist each other in the practical sphere of daily life.

The function of the hands also relates to the yin/yang
principle and the Taoist physiology of the left and right sides
of the brain and their different functions. Generally, the left
side of the brain controls the sequential processes of logic,
analysis, rational and scientific behavior, the right side of
the body and the special processes of institution, creativity
and dreaming. A dominance in either side of the brain is
apparent by observing the behavior and actions of an individual or nation. The two sides of the brain dominate the
two sides of the body in intersecting ways. The left brain
governs the right side of the body and the right brain
governs the left side of the body. "Military aggression" can
be associated with an overly dominant left side of the brain
and "the strong right." Since consideration and sensitivity
are associated with the right side of the brain, it is easy to
see how "gentle people value the soft left hand." The Integral

Way is the balance and cooperation of both hemispheres of the brain: "Use upright measures to govern the country, use a surprising approach to win the battle, and lead the world using both ways; do not apply interference or disturbance." These ancient discoveries of the specialized knowledge about the function of the brain in acupuncture practice has been accurately utilized in natural diagnosis and acupuncture practice since the Stone Age. Right and left side brain controls are of utmost importance in acupuncture treatment. For example, in the case of someone who has become paralyzed or twisted, acupuncture needles would be applied to the side opposite that of the paralyzed side.

Pulse diagnosis in natural healing uses the different functions of the left/right sides of the brain which influence pulsation, thereby yielding the secrets of the body. The most accurate time for reading the pulse is early morning, before any mental or physical activity has had a chance to disturb or change the pulse rate.

In ancient times, some Taoists also used pulse reading as the basis for telling a person's fortune and predicting what would happen in the near or distant future. They knew that the development of both sides of a person's brain divulged the secrets and decisive factors of one's life. This same principle is also applied in palm reading, where the lines of the palm tell the secrets of the brain and thus the influence the lines have over one's whole life. When one's customary patterns of life change, the lines of one's palm change correspondingly.

Ancient integral cultural development was based on the natural reality of balance between the right and left sides of the human brain. Today that balance has obviously been lost. The modern "right-hand" culture of logic is accepted, while the ancient "left-hand" intuitive cultural achievement is mistakenly rejected.

That is more mystical, but to reflect on a more worldly level, the natural evolution of the human race in both the eastern and western hemispheres can be observed. Their tendencies and habits are interestingly contrasted with each other. Since Earth is shaped like the brain, the different developments of the east and west sides of the globe should also serve each other in beneficial ways. However, it appears that the left side of the brain is overused in today's society. The Tai Chi symbol 🌓 expresses complete balance of both sides. It resembles the brain, with even right and left halves, and the globe of the earth, with balanced east and west hemispheres. This symbol of balance, development and integration can be applied to all things and all events.

In Taoist guidance for human life, the left hand expresses harmony in the world as well as in human cultures. Earth is not only a mixture of soil, rocks and minerals, but is also a vast living organism; it is a life. Abuse of the earth by people is a type of suicidal behavior of the human race.

The sky is your brain, the earth is your body. Both express the integrity of your life nature. Damage to one's integrity may also be caused by specialization. A well-trained athlete takes a long time to excel at his or her special event. One may be good at javelin throwing, hammer throwing, discus throwing, and so forth; however, the result of this type of special training generally makes the arm and leg of one side thicker than the arm and leg on the other side. In some situations, such an imbalance can seriously influence one's brain, organs, personality and total health. People who train with iron-made devices and use machines for building their muscles probably experience a mechanical reaction in their personalities, due to lack of naturalness and flexibility of their bodies and minds.

Not only do physical training and sports produce unnatural results, but much learning, specific training and some professions also produce adverse effects. These effects often limit one's capabilities and interactions with others. Specialists often see only the trees without seeing the forest.

In order to achieve harmony, it is necessary to balance and integrate yin and yang as one unit. This balance is the subtle yet sustaining power of the universe. Every positive manifestation in the universe comes forth as the result of the creative, harmonious union of yin and yang energies, and each manifestation has its own unique energy arrangement and pattern of movement.

Following the inherent order of the universe, which is the wholeness of nature of your life, results in harmony and balance. Opposing the principle of natural order causes destruction. Anything that is one-sided is incomplete. Balance can also be illustrated by the operation of the Tai Chi principle as it is performed in a special Taoist type of exercise which is also called T'ai Chi. But here, I do not mean the Taoist gentle exercise. I mean the universal movement produces the Tai Chi principle, the law of universal movement and life. Tai Chi is universal movement, a continual sequence of yin and yang movements. That is how T'ai Chi Chuan as an exercise originated as a form of integral cultivation, from the universal movement. T'ai Chi exercise is used by Taoists as one way to cultivate chi. All of the movements performed in this type of exercise, as an expression of yin and yang, are balanced as nature itself. Nothing should be excessive. If there is upward movement, there must be downward movement. If there is movement to the right, there must also be movement to the left. Inhalation and exhalation should also be coordinated to maintain balance. One can not only practice the balancing type of movements in one's practice of T'ai Chi exercise, but it is also possible to integrate the principles of Tai Chi into one's own life. That is to follow Tao. By drawing on the understanding of all movements brought about by oneself and the vast nature, one will be able to lead a balanced, integrated life.

In the above discussion, my focus is to explain the Tai Chi principle as the universal reality. Tai Chi movement is used as one of the examples of this ultimate law. The universe consists of yang and yin, two types of energy as two types of movement, to start its dualistic development. But to cultivate Tao, is to go back to the oneness from your dualistic position.

Chapter 3

Self-Cultivation - The Golden Key
To the Gate of Universal Eternal Light

The hexagram Chun ䷂ means to assemble, station, or stockpile. The yang energy is blocked in both the upper and lower trigrams. In the lower trigram, ☳, the first yang line is stopped by the two yin lines. In the upper trigram, ☵, the yang line is limited by the yin lines on both sides of it. In this situation, the growth of yang energy is needed more than immediate movement. Therefore, cultivation should be applied in order to accumulate the yang, original energy.

It can be said that cultivating chi, practicing subtle virtue and attaining enlightenment are one and the same. When we do things, we also learn them. When we practice things, we also nurture ourselves. The process is almost indivisible. However, it is necessary to keep a balance among the three. On the one hand, we should always be diligent about the cultivation of bodily fitness, healthy attitudes and the correct practice of virtue and capability in our work. At the same time, we should put our cultivation to good use. Both sides of one's outlook and nature need to be balanced; this is the principle of cultivating oneself or training students in the Taoist way. The development of our capability, integrity, uprightness and efficiency comes from the constant work of cultivation. Without cultivation, one never has the chance to reflect on what one's life has been.

The effect of your self-cultivation shows who you really are. If you do not take the chance to correct or improve yourself, you will stay at the same undeveloped level. For example, if you are interested in learning T'ai Chi exercise, you can learn the form in three to four months and then have the ability to do the whole thing. However, to arrive at the level of mastery - knowing all the details, correct breathing and corresponding internal energy movements - it takes daily practice over many years. Some people, however, do not have the correct focus while the do the practice, so they derive less benefit from the exercise. What matters most is the internal work. By internal work, I mean the internal cooperation while you do the external exercise. T'ai Chi exercise is not limited to superficial movement. Self-cultivation is also one way to deepen your capacity for appreciation of the subtle energy. The highest appreciation is the appreciation of nature's simplicity and plainness. If you have not developed the capability of deep appreciation, then your life runs down wrong alleys, and everything loses its real meaning, including your personal life. To lose the meaning of your personal life is dangerous. It can cause great self-indulgence or even death.

In the Taoist way of life, work is important. Before you reach enlightenment, you should use all your energy to break through the darkness. This is the pursuit of enlightenment. Because you are not enlightened, you live in darkness. Beginners often think they are enlightened, but the teachings of all great masters and spiritual books are usually completely beyond the ones who claim to understand them. This is like taking the tusks of an ancient elephant, so rare, valuable and beautiful, and putting them on a dog's mouth. The dog is still a dog. You can put the tusks of an elephant on your own mouth or you can read all the great works of the ancient masters, but without enlightenment you are still exactly the same.

People sometimes think that by staying in their present positions, without self-improvement, they can become immortal. What kind of immortal do you wish to become? Perhaps you can become an immortal bug! Improve yourself while you set up your goal. I hope that some of the things that you read in this book can motivate you to find your good points and develop them further, so that you can improve your own life and benefit the world.

What is enlightenment? What is truth? What makes it so interesting? In the latter part of his life Confucius said, "If in the morning I know the truth, I am enlightened. Then, if that very evening I am dying, I am satisfied." Are you satisfied?

Enlightenment is personal. Because people live different lives, how much wisdom an individual can produce varies. The amount of spiritual attainment derived from reading my books varies for different people, too. It is not for me to tell you what your enlightenment will be; it is for you to tell me enlightenment is after you have worked with my books and/or videotapes.

Equal to the importance of enlightenment in Taoist cultivation is the gaining of chi. You may think you already have chi. Surely you do. Don't you think that poison oak has chi also? All life has chi, but different people accumulate different kinds of chi in their lives. What is really valuable is to accumulate and refine your personal chi and transform it into divine immortal chi, which is the most refined, supreme chi of all. If you had only a little of that chi, your whole personality would be different. Having divine chi is like being a person who has a piece of jade in his bosom yet wears coarse clothing.

What kind of chi do you have? Through enlightenment, through the practice of virtue and through practical and technical cultivation, you can gain the highest chi. Without this, you are like a donkey who bears a golden saddle. You may think you are enlightened, but you are still a donkey. A spiritually achieved person who has the most refined, supreme chi is a flying horse; nobody can even catch sight of his shadow.

Practically speaking, supreme chi can be gained through correct cultivation and the consistent practice of virtue; these surely change one's being. As one's sensitivity to the natural flow of life increases, one's personal thought patterns and inner awareness begins to harmonize with truth, and enlightenment naturally follows. Through the practice of virtue and correct cultivation, one can gain the supreme chi.

The way is so simple. Work on your enlightenment in order to change your darkness. This does not mean that enlightenment itself has such a high value; the actual value of enlightening oneself is the removal of darkness.

How do you take away darkness formed by many lifetimes so that you finally become enlightened? By working hard to become spiritual? Unfortunately, for many, this is like putting the cart before the horse and can even increase the darkness. "Rather than trying hard to become spiritual, you just take your own assets and skills and develop them to the point of human perfection. As you become a more refined individual from doing this, you shall see the new enlightened person. As you work to eliminate your darkness, your spiritual eyes will naturally open. Equally important in personal life is the consistent practice of virtue and development of a personal code of conduct in accord with what is positive and good, vital and enlivening. Your virtue is the energy and fragrance of your life and your golden key to crystal clear vision. If your personality has become contaminated, work on cleansing it. Be assured that when you change yourself inside, it is naturally expressed outside. No need to buy and wear a golden saddle while you are still a donkey. There is no enlightened donkey. There are only enlightened human individuals. You just need to become different internally, to affect a change in your external life.

If you understand the above, you know that becoming enlightened and working with the Taoist methods is not a matter of faith. Religious faith is connected with what and how you believe. Faith in its negative aspect works by blind belief. It is like being taught that fire is cold. If you believe that fire is cold, even when burned by it, if you have survived, you will still think it is cold. The teaching of Tao does not promote rigid, blind faith which can induce psychological or hypnotic effects that are fragile in truth and lacking in durability. The teaching of Tao is a matter of understanding and doing. The teaching of Tao inspires, enlightens and opens you up for higher integration. After spending some time studying Taoist materials and learning some Taoist practices, you might become an authority over both mundane and eternal life. Taoism teaches openness. It is through openness that a person can reach the essence in order to develop one's being. The teaching of Tao is the path of open-ended growth.

The secret of eternal life is beyond conceptual exploration. It could almost be considered as a scientific secret, because it takes a scientific kind of approach to learn it. It can be expressed by riddles, puzzles and metaphors. No wise person can decode them or fit the pieces of understanding together into the whole picture unless he is a real student, guided by divine immortal selection. When talking about the level of learning that is represented by the words "attaining immortality", it is not only extremely difficult for a pupil to find a teacher, it is also difficult for an achieved one to find the right person to whom he can pass the knowledge of divine immortality. It is not a matter of family ties, as the relationship of father and son. It is a matter of being the "right one."

The *Tao Teh Ching* says that Tao is invisible, inaudible and untouchable. This description is appropriate for the spiritually undeveloped, but to those who are spiritually developed the truth is visible, audible and touchable. It always exists. The key of the teaching of Tao can be included in such a way. As all forms are the form of Tao, no particular form can be insisted on as being Tao.

Chapter 4

The Light in One's Personality

Following what is right
*   is like being part of a stream*
*   flowing toward the ocean.*
Keeping one's innate virtue
*   is the true foundation of happiness.*
Through practicing great virtue,
*   one can change one's personality*
*   and alter one's life.*
One's life will then be peaceful and long.
Persevere in doing things
*   only of a giving and constructive nature,*
*   and your heart will become pure and free of*
*   negativity.*

Extend the care you cultivate in your own family
*   to all things and creatures surrounding your house,*
*   such as the plants and animals.*
When you make an error, correct it as best you can,
*   and do not harbor guilt within.*
Be earnest in all you do.
Soften your disposition,
*   and be thorough in your good conduct.*
Do not do anything that cannot be exposed to daylight;
*   it will be seen in the subtle realm of Heaven*
*   as a flash of lightning.*
See virtue as your main goal in life,
*   and enjoy helping others.*
Never let an opportunity to help pass.
To be honest, faithful, trustworthy and sincere
*   is to be carefree.*
If your virtue and your talents are equally good,
*   you are a superior person.*
If you want your good deeds to be seen by others,
*   the good is lost.*

Do good for the sake of doing good,
  and do not expect anything in return.
Take care of little things;
  be diligent in caring for life.
Educate others by setting the right example,
  not by preaching.
Do not promise lightly;
  and when you promise, keep it.
Never tire of the pursuit
  of the actualization of your inherent virtue.
Turn your mind to what is deep,
  abandon the shallow.
Develop a strong heart with the virtues of
  benevolence, humanitarianism, justice and kindness.
Care for all without partiality;
  be sincere and guileless.
Maintain right conduct, control passion.
As one's virtues increase daily, so will one's health.
Do not express any negative energy
  in thought, word or action.
Humility is the root of virtue,
  but being overly humble is artful and false.
Exercising excessive pride causes decrease,
  exercising humility causes increase.
It is better to acknowledge your faults
  than to tell a lie.
Righteousness in thought, word and action
  is how the upright person preserves his integrity.
Of all vices, lewdness is the worst offender.
Do not deceive others in word, action or thought;
  know that the subtle energy responds accordingly.
Remember the law of attraction;
  what you are, think and express,
  attracts corresponding energy.
Without fail, you will meet the results
  of your positive or negative thoughts and actions.
Do not separate spiritual practices
  from your conduct in daily life;
  they should move on one channel
  and be tuned into each other.

Burning incense, sitting in meditation,
  and not correcting your behavior
  is perilous and leads nowhere.
Always remember that your true nature is virtuous,
  and by practicing diligently the virtues of life,
  you will reach purity and clarity of being.

Chapter 5

The Path to Spiritual Unification

As you walk ever more firmly on the path of Tao,
*   you will leave impurity and lust behind.*
Needs that once were, are simply no longer.
If at first the six sense organs
*   become enemies and obstructions,*
*   in time they will prove the wealth*
*   of your cultivation.*
Be sincere in the Tao,
*   and there will be a change in your body and heart.*

Observe these six dangers closely:

*   One: Do not confuse what is*
*   with what you want it to be.*
*   Your will cannot preside.*
*   (Besides, it is not yours).*
*   You cannot change the direction of things.*
*   To try is to intrude.*

*   Two: Release all concepts*
*   that come into your mind.*
*   Do not cling to any of them.*

*   Three: There is nothing that is necessary. Nothing.*

*   Four: The sovereignty of Nature is just that.*
*   Do not impose on it nor act in place of its authority.*

*   Five: Do not rebel and challenge the law of Nature.*
*   This is foolish and destructive.*

*   Six: Remember, your mind is not your own.*
*   It is a gift of life from Nature.*
*   It is imperative to use it positively, constructively.*
*   To do otherwise, to use it for worry, anger*
*   or negativity, is to abuse the mighty gift.*

A mind united with Tao
   is devoid of thoughts that are a constant ramble,
   even thoughts pondering utmost wonders
   and mysteries.
Sincere cultivation is done naturally, easily,
   in the here and now.
Only in calmness can one see infinity.
So, if you are a beginner,
   close your eyes and search inside your soul,
   head and body upright, keeping the heart at peace,
   the mind calm.
Discontinue showing a false front
   to others and to yourself,
   whether in your way of living or thinking.
It is not you and thus is dishonest
   to your true nature.
Keep your integrity,
   no need to search the outside world for your soul.
Again and again you will see,
   it is with the pure mind only
   that you can become one with Tao.
It is with the pure mind only
   that you can bask in the radiance
   of the true spiritual sun.
In this way, you will be allowed
   to be the seed of a whole being.

Chapter 6

The Paradox of Truth

All opposites are united. A view that has integrated all opposites is balanced and can therefore be of help in reaching the truth. Living with a balanced spirit allows one to avoid life's many diversions.

All polarities become the elements of life. This is illustrated by our paired feet and hands. Each one supports the other with every new step or movement. With the integration of polarities, one's life can regain its original balance.

One cannot expect beauty to last forever, goodness to remain constant, or the high never to fall. Every day is a "fair weather" day. Excitement is built up by each ordinary moment; the climax, by low tones. A Taoist would stay with the ordinary moments, and does not expect excitement. A Taoist would work for the steady progress with the low tones. He does not look for the climax. Success is contained in every common minute. The recognition of regularity, plainness, ordinariness and usualness is the fundamental element for achieving a balanced way.

By embracing integral oneness and dissolving discriminating opposites, one can maintain natural-born flexibility and thus live deeply within one's own spirit. This practice will allow one to transcend all worldly attachments and the unhealthy, contradictory, dualistic sphere of the human world. Thus, one may achieve immortality.

Spiritual truth is sometimes paradoxical. The following story is my own personal experience in the pursuit of enlightenment. When I was young and engaged in the activities of youth, my father always reminded me of the importance of achieving enlightenment. I told my father, "I am bright already. What enlightenment should I look for?"

My father said, "The enlightenment you should have at first is to know that you are behind the darkness of your brightness."

I had not yet discovered that I was "behind the darkness of my brightness," as my father said. I thought I was smart.

Taking pride in my smartness was probably my darkness. I finally realized my own darkness and began working on it to discover real enlightenment. After many years of cultivation, hard life and difficult times, I eventually felt enlightened. I went to my father and told him, "I don't need to look for the truth anymore. All truth is here, now! For people of starvation, the truth is to eat. For people of over-consumption, to eat less is the truth. For people of poverty, to be rich is the truth. For people of illness, to be well is the truth. For people of leisure, to work is the truth. For people of constant work, to relax is the truth. For people of a rigidly organized life, flexibility is the truth. For people of sloppiness, to become well-disciplined is the truth. For people of spiritual underdevelopment, to pursue enlightenment is the truth. For people of deep spiritual development, helping to improve the confused world is the truth.

"The truth is always in the polar opposite. We call Polaris the 'Northern' star, because we are south of it. If we change our position, we see and name things differently. This shows the relativity of yin and yang. An achieved one can embody all truth with his single being. At the same time, all such truth is irrelevant to him."

My father said, "Tell me how can you embody all truth with your single being and, at the same time, make all such truth irrelevant?"

I pondered this question carefully and responded, "All such truth I mentioned is the use or function of the truth. It is not the body or the entity of truth. All uses of truth are specific expressions of it. Every moment and activity may be an expression of truth. Therefore, as the ancient achieved one said, 'One cannot depart from the truth for a single second.' All uses of truth are the truth. At the same time, since all uses of the truth are merely expressions of truth, they are irrelevant to the independence and wholeness of the body of truth."

"Can the use and body of truth be separated as different existing entities?" my father asked.

"No," I replied. "The use of truth and the body of truth cannot be separated. When one of them is perceived, the other also appears. When one of them is disregarded, the other also disappears."

"Well," my father said, "in this way, the existence of truth must have acknowledgement, otherwise it cannot be independent. Is this what you meant? Furthermore, is it not possible for truth to be disregarded or unnoticed, my beloved one?"

"No, sir. If it is the truth, it must always be independent, transcendental and absolute. Otherwise, how can it be truth?"

"My son, in your previous statement, you said that for people who are starving, the truth is to eat; for people of thirst, the truth is to drink and so forth. Now, may I ask you, if to eat and to drink are the truth, then are hunger and thirst the mother of truth? If hunger and thirst are the mother or substance of truth, they should be higher than truth itself. The substance of truth is immutable and unchangeable. What, then, is above your truth?"

After this discussion, I continued to work on the amazing topic of truth. I was up and down with the truth. I was shaken by the pursuit of the truth. At the same time, I was also strongly enchanted by the experience of being enlightened by the truth. I was at work day and night with this puzzle. Finally, I developed two theories. First, that enlightenment is some place you can reach alone, without anyone's help. I called this the "theory of self-reaching." The second theory was this: even if you have had an experience of enlightenment, you cannot share it with anyone go there again, because enlightenment is a climax of the plateau of spiritual experience. The exception is with a like-minded person. I called this the "theory of non-transmissibility of enlightenment."

I held to these two points to define the experience of enlightenment by truth. As for myself, I thought that I was already at a certain level of enlightenment. Before my next meeting with my father, I hoped to do some further preparation, just in case he gave me more trouble with the "truth." Interestingly enough, the night before our meeting, I received an important dream.

In the dream, I was walking in a place where there were two cliffs with a deep ravine between them. I was on the higher side of the ravine. On the other side, I could hear a woman of late middle age talking to a young man about her adoration of a religious "star" that had been shining for more than a thousand years. She was saying that this star's life was the only living truth, and it would enlighten all followers with the truth.

Since I was on the other shore, I hurried to go over to her because I wished to correct the false belief she had. I wanted to tell her that every person is the life of truth, and at the same time, no one is the truth itself. Truth is not presentable by, or as, anybody or anything. To do so would damage the truth. Truth is Truth; it cannot change hands.

As I approached her, but before I could correct her, I noticed that on the same shore in another place a man was talking to some other people about the truth. He felt that he had a better way of presenting it. Again I thought I must go there quickly and stop him with my "theory of non-transmissibility," that the real truth cannot be passed. When one wishes to describe truth, it is no longer the moment one experienced as the truth. Or, when one experiences the desire to describe truth, that desire ends the experience of truth. I went over to him to convey my thought: "If you hold this way of talking about the truth, the truth will no longer be the truth, but only words." However, when I was close enough to him, I discovered by the smell of his breath that he was drunk. Immediately, I decided that what he had achieved must be alcohol truth. Before I could begin my explanation he greeted me and invited me to his cellar to enjoy some good wine with him. This friendly gesture made it awkward for me to immediately and straightforwardly pass my message to him. I also began to feel some difficulty because he seemed beyond my help. By this time, he was so busy with his wine that he had no time for anything else, and when he offered me the wine, I could not drink it since I discovered I had a toothache. At this time I also discovered my shoelace was loose and needed to be tied.

Suddenly I awoke and could not sleep anymore. I wondered about the meaning of this dream. It seemed to me

that in spiritual achievement the problem is not enlightenment itself, but the "transmission" of enlightenment. The
matters of enlightenment and darkness are on two different
shores. It is easy for a person on the high side to descend
to the low side, but it is difficult to communicate with people
on the low side. Also, on the low side of a steep ravine,
darkness influences people differently. This had just been
illustrated in my dream.

I thought carefully about which part of my dream was
connected with the ultimate truth. The next morning, when
I faced my father, he said in a clear voice, "When your
shoelace is loose, tie it. When you have a toothache, keep
away from drinking. In the freshness of the early morning,
gather the chi. During the brightness of the day practice
subtle virtue. In the darkness of midnight maintain enlightenment. People of deviation seem to have many chances to
expound the truth, but truth never gives the Integral One a
chance to express it."

Chapter 7

The Restoration of Normalcy

After ages of departing from the right way through insistently following its own will, mankind has lost its natural balance. Man's mind has become distorted and his very life untrue. Instead of having his energy centered and focused as it should be, it often floats upward and scatters, stimulating one or another of the sensory organs. This imbalance manifests as being self-centered, boastful, envious, jealous, quarrelsome, as gossiping, raving about the opposite sex, taking things too easily, assuming to be learned and having contempt for the stupid, finding fault with others, having an excess of desire and corrupting the morals of others or being overly ambitious.

The negativity of most people can be changed and refined through cultivation as self-awareness unfolds and self-completion evolves. One should neither be inert nor frivolous, but follow a normal balance. To hold fast to the waves of your negative energy is dangerous. Return to the right way before you go out too far into the open sea. Return to the shore of positivity and constructive creativity. This safe shore is to be found in the transformation of your own energy elements and through spiritual evolution as taught in Taoism. Taoism teaches that physical and mental well-being are the foundation for high spiritual attainment. This is called the restoration of normalcy. Normalcy is a good condition. Normalcy is when everything is in the right position and right function. Normalcy is not a special occasion that expresses trouble. That is Taoist normalcy.

Chapter 8

Natural Light in Relationships

The inner essence of the universe is benevolent.
People, within their true natures,
*   functioning as a microcosm of the universe,*
*   are also benevolent and should, therefore,*
*   cherish humanity in their hearts.*
Use tolerance and patience toward others.
Be loyal and forgiving, warm and sincere.
Extend your harmonious energy to others.
Do not complain,
*   so as not to pass on your negativity.*
Approach everyone with an open mind
*   and without pushing yourself forward,*
*   but do not bare your heart*
*   when meeting for the first time.*

Judge yourself well and others moderately.
Be forgiving, and forgive fully and frankly.
There is always a good reason
*   to forget another's faults.*
Remember, even the sages were not faultless.
Keep your tongue quiet
*   so as not to provoke arguments.*
Leave room for your own repentance
*   and compensation*
*   in every affair.*
Be flexible and yielding, and do not quarrel.
Bear an insult and keep your dignity.
To repress a moment of anger
*   can save you much regret.*
Strive to be selfless, not self-centered.
A self-centered person expects favors from others,
*   while a selfless person gives to others*
*   and never asks anything in return.*

Win people's hearts, and do not impose
upon their wills.

With affinity, people will meet each other from
a great distance.
Without affinity, even when face to face,
two people might never truly meet.
When people are of the same virtuous mind,
their integrity will cut metal.
Do not have intimate dealings with unvirtuous people
whose words mean little
and whose actions are indecisive.
Do not nourish an unfaithful person.
If one associates with unvirtuous people,
one will be negatively influenced by them.
Be fraternal and friendly to everyone,
but keep your own balanced nature
whole and untouched.
Do not speak of another's shortcomings at any time.
If you respect others,
they will in turn respect you.
Be humble and willing to serve people
whenever you can.
Thus is the nature and the absolute virtue
of the universe.

Chapter 9

Taming the Wild Horse Within Yourself

Bridle the mind, for it is like a wild horse. It needs to be tamed. First one has to know it is there, running on the plain. Then try to catch it, ride it, lead it by the reins and be watchful of its movements all the time. With firmness, gentleness and patience, the horse will be tamed and the master known.

One has to practice the healthy way daily and unconditionally to achieve lasting results. Without daily practice, the little progress one makes will wither away quickly. Thus, be constantly aware of the movement of the mind. If it is negative, lazy or inconsiderate, subtly but firmly change the channel on the mind's screen to a positive and giving direction. At first it may seem unnatural not to follow the impulse of the mind, since one is used to following the self-willed mind without question. But being impulsive is not the same as being spontaneous. Spontaneity is a refined state of attunement with life in its united form. Gradually, one's effort brings one to a higher state of energy. One's mind becomes pure, little by little, and one's actions become spontaneously virtuous.

It takes many years to purify the mind. Have courage and trust the positive nature of the universe and the positive nature of one's own being. Practice taming the wild horse daily; never skip a day.

Chapter 10

The Natural Light in Everyday Life

If you are about to do something,
  consider its disadvantages first
  and see if you can do it
  without causing the problems.
Use caution before taking action.
Restrain yourself from moving too fast
  and from dissipating your energy
  in too many directions.
Do not meddle in someone else's affairs;
  it will only complicate your life
  and bring confusion.
Preserve the serenity of your nature
  by observing the multiple activities of life
  and not participating in whatever
  would destroy the day's serenity.
As a spectator, you can see clearly
  that the participants are often lost in the maze.

Stay with the oneness of all things.
Do not talk more than necessary.
Do not let your mind run from this subject to that.
Walk on the balanced path of Tao
  and you will be preserved.
Take moderation as your guide;
  even happiness should not be enjoyed to excess.
Cherish self-control
  and hold fast to the subtle law of nature.

Do not be a servant to material things.
Simplify your life by doing away with things;
  do not accumulate them.
Give away what your cherish most,
  and your desire for material things will diminish.

Be prepared for the future.

If you are prepared for difficulties,
  they become easy to overcome.
In taking action, be far thinking.
Consider the consequences at all levels.
If your motive is selfish or will harm others,
  restrain from taking action.
When you have attained your objective,
  use caution and do not overdo it.
Be heedful in the beginning to ensure a good ending.

Always try to help yourself
  before you ask help from others;
But never feel too proud
  to ask for assistance if you need it.

Keep your mind clear and you will be able
  to manage your affairs in good order.
A clear mind is an uncluttered mind;
  make it one-pointed and direct.

Manage public affairs with selfless judgment
  and fairness.
One must display honesty, generosity and earnestness.
Do not deceive people;
  the heart knows and cannot be deceived.

Be gentle in doing right; do not be violent.
Be sure that your conduct is in harmony
  with your understanding,
  even in small matters.

The essence of work is diligence.
 A successful life depends on
    doing the right thing at the right time
    and obeying the cosmic law.
Blessings come in many ways.
Do not look for happiness, and you will be content.

Continuously remove negativity within yourself.
One's good life is decided by one's virtue
 and a clean mind.
To endure difficulty, quit complaining.

To endure vexation and annoyance,
 avoid bitter comment.
If your mind is always occupied by distress,
 good fortune is sure to evade you.
When things get to their worst,
 they can only get better.
When something reaches its limit,
 it has to return to its opposite.
This is the Tai Chi of events.
Avoid involvement with people who are suspicious,
 easily pleased or angered.
Listen only to proposals of a balanced view.
Walk away from idle talk.
Unite with people of outstanding character.
Collective purpose forms a fortress.
In uniting harmonized energies, we gather strength.

Chapter 11

The Natural Light in General Life

The five blessings of life are:
    health, longevity, virtuous behavior,
    prosperity and a natural death.
The five constant virtues are:
    propriety, benevolence, righteousness,
    wisdom and faith.
Those who live in accord with
    the universal subtle law are preserved.

Aim at human and spiritual nobility.
There is one word that we can use as a motto
    for our entire life: reciprocity.
What we do not want to be done to ourselves,
    we must not do to others.
The more we give to others,
    the more abundant our lives become.
In helping people and caring for life,
    our own lives will be rewarding.

On entering a country, do not do what is forbidden;
    follow the customs.
On entering a house, respect the taste of the family;
    in this way there will be no improper behavior.
A wise man is free of perplexities,
    because he understands what is right and wrong.
A virtuous man is free of anxieties,
    because he tries his best in all undertakings
    and regards failure as a means
    to strengthen his character.
A man of courage is free from fear,
    because he strongly believes in his goals,
    regardless of the difficulties.

Do not desire to have things done quickly
    if they cannot be done thoroughly;
Success in work is founded on thoroughness.

Do not be greedy of small advantages,
and great projects can be accomplished.
Be eager to inquire when in doubt;
one who does not learn from others
will remain ignorant.
The learned man may not be wise,
and the wise man may not be learned.
Be aware of the difference between wisdom
and learned knowledge.

True fulfillment in life is derived from hardship.
One can only appreciate the joy of fulfilled
responsibility after shouldering the burden.
The best strategists are not impulsive;
the best winners are not quarrelsome;
the best rulers are not arrogant.
Things have their beginnings and their endings;
events have their causes and their outcome.
To know which should be first
and which should be last
will bring one nearer to the truth of life.

Live with virtue and abide with the laws of nature.
Do not shallowly care for your own comfort
and indulgences.
A man of leisure will never find success.
Be efficient in work and careful in speech.
Correct your faults and be humble.

Never tire of studying and practicing
the right way of life.
If you do not practice and study,
you will not grow to completeness.
Although the job is simple,
one can never complete it without working.
Although the distance is short,
one can never reach the goal without walking.

There is no definite route to success or failure,
as they are very intricate.

*The reason some succeed and others fail
    is that those who persist in a positive direction
    succeed, while those who do not will fail.*

*When Heaven is going to confer an important task
    on someone, first it makes his mind suffer
    and labors his body with heavy tasks.
It will present hardships,
    and defeat all his undertakings.
Through all these trials,
    it strengthens his mind and will
    so that he may overcome all difficulties.*

*If you want to enjoy a long and fulfilling life
    supported by the energy of Heaven,
    diligently cultivate virtuous action.
There is a right way and a wrong way to live.
The virtuous way may lead to disadvantage,
    but victory is assured.
The unvirtuous way may lead to prosperity,
    but failure is inevitable.
Take care to proceed on the right path.
If you stray, know that there is always a safe shore
    to which you can return.*

*If one's heart is wrongly pursuing evil,
    then even though it has not been accomplished,
    bad fortune will follow.
Consider the success and failure of others as your own;
    share in their fortune and misfortune.
Do not aggressively or unrighteously
    expose the faults of others,
    nor boast of your own excellence.
Do not hold a grudge toward anyone.
Live with humility.*

Chapter 12

The Sacred Light of Natural Life

The universe never dies
because it maintains its eternal constancy.
All creatures die
because they allow their external environment
to continually change their own natures
and their virtues.
Some people are attracted by the outside world
and do not feel content or sufficient
within their own natures.
They follow what is attractive to them.
They always want to be something or someone else
and, so doing, depart from their own good natures.
One dies every minute one departs
from one's true nature.
Every minute is a new life to a true being.

As I awakened in Tao, I came to know:
with Tao we receive life;
Tao is the eternal way;
Tao is the constancy of the universe;
Tao is the origin of our vitality;
Tao is the enduring spirit of life.

Moving about in the spiritual world,
I abide with the eternal spirit.
I am content with my own nature.
The harmonized energy of the universe supports me
and I live firmly with the eternal Tao.
I can alter confusion and dangerous situations
by abiding in the true power of the
subtle virtue of the universe.
I follow a regular, normal way of life,
avoiding all extremes, excesses
and extravagances.
I am plain, simple and true.

I never allow myself to daydream
  or wish to be a saint or other exalted being,
  only a being of wholeness.
I walk the Way,
  without concern for my future, past or present.
My emotions are softened, my desires few.
I keep my spirit untouched,
  my mind clear and detached,
  my body still and upright.
All my actions have a deep respect
  for the original stillness of the universe.
I use non-action or non-deviation
  as a gateway to true work.
Though peacefully engaged in life,
  I abide in the infinite simplicity of Tao.
This is the way to perpetual peace,
  true beauty, happiness and joy.
This is the secret of a Taoist natural life.

Chapter 13

Spiritual Function of Heaven and Earth

Create positive influences
  for the needs of our fellow men.
From this we must not walk away.
Have compassion for the inferior world.
Becoming one of the spiritual healing lights,
  you provide a model and spiritual influence
  for all spiritual beings.
The radiance of your smile, your speech,
  your conduct and your way of life,
  weaves a cohesive and beneficial medicine
  for all sick minds and bodies.

Maintaining kindness, generosity and grace
  is the heritage of our Heavenly kinship.
The virtue of Heaven and earth
  gives birth to all things.
The nature of Heaven and earth
  leads us to our Heavenly home.
Through compassion we not only enjoy eternity,
  we unite with the positive energy of all life.

Worldly people desire life and fear death.
But, fear it or not, physical death is certain.
Immortality can only be achieved
  through many deaths.
As the impulsive mind dies,
  the shadow of life and death can be seen
  as the surface activity of non-conscious awareness,
  for nothing is ever really born or destroyed.
The luminosity of pure mind
  comes only with the death of desire.
As the mind dies, your spirit comes alive,
  realizing an unusual majestic light.

The sons and daughters of impurity
  count worldly enjoyment as blessings.

In doing so, they block the channels of super energy.
They cannot see death hiding
   in the pleasures they seek.
Though death many not be immediate,
   these pursuits sap their vital essences
   and carry the odors of a corpse.
Only the true sons and daughters of
   Heavenly, whole beings
   know the wonderful principle
   of receiving life through death.

Chapter 14

Stay With the Fundamental
After Achieving the Great

There is nothing more worthwhile in life than to follow Tao. Possessing wealth, fame, position, power, intelligence, wisdom, beauty, etc., does not really matter. The most magnificent of all things is Tao. Though Tao cannot be possessed, it can be embodied. As stated in Chapter 25 of the *Tao Teh Ching*:

> *"Humanity takes the example of Earth*
> *   to stabilize itself.*
> *Earth takes the example of Heaven*
> *   to rotate itself.*
> *Heaven takes the example of Tao*
> *   to purify itself.*
> *Tao takes the example of itself*
> *   to integrate and disintegrate*
> *   all things and all lives."*

What do the luxuries of life, ornamental knowledge, psychological toys, social and religious vanities all mean to human life? They only serve your emotion, they do not benefit your soul. Rather than seek them in excessive quantity, value your plain life. Do not do things that cause you to lose your original perfect balance. This is called "wu wei" (non-doing).

Although it does not matter if you do something, it does matter if you overdo it. This is called "wei wu wei" (do the non-doing). These are two important guidelines from the *Tao Teh Ching*.

Mind, desires, entrails and bones are the main constitution of human life. Do not let the mind exhaust that which supports the body. If the mind is overused, the entrails become weakened. If one has too many desires, the bones become hardened and the marrow dried.

The lopsided, dualistic-mindedness of people who lack spiritual integration becomes an obstacle in achieving or maintaining the wholeness of mind and spirit. Thus, battles and wars never end, within and without. It is impossible to attain inner peace or outer harmony without the achievement of mental and spiritual self-integration. This is to say that whole-mindedness must be put above all the philosophical and religious conceptions that have been the source of strife among people and have led to mental and spiritual separation from the absolute truth. In other words, it is only by clearing your mind of whatever you have been taught that will bring you to wholeness.

Chapter 15

Be Unaffected by the World Mixture

The wise person avoids having interest
in that which is extreme.
When he knows something,
he knows that he knows it.
When he does not know something,
he is also aware of that.
In this way he preserves true knowledge.
When he experiences trouble,
he uses it to develop his wisdom.
He uses roundness in thinking,
and squareness in conduct.
He does not murmur against Heaven
or blame other people.
In observing the possible movement of things,
he develops the brightness of his mind.
Cordiality and gratitude
are the assets of his life.
He is of a most natural and pleasing appearance,
and his mind has a high degree of ease and peace.
He can be thus because
he keeps his mind dispassionate
and unaffected by the cares of the world.
If you have respect for the high spirits
of the ancient sages
and think of them as if
they were in front of you,
They will then respond to you
as friends and guides.
In this way, you can connect with
the highest realm of the universe.

Chapter 16

Seek the Deep Reality of Life
While Living in the Shallow World

In times of ease,
  one with a deep vision of life
  follows the way of immortality.
Love not the world of colored dust.
One hundred years pass in an instant.
In the time it takes to snap your fingers,
  we live and die.
Our temporary existence
  is as significant as a dew drop.
Yesterday a man rode his horse through the streets;
  today he lies sleeping in his coffin.
This is the glamour of life.

Like so many autumn leaves,
  all the stories of a man's life one day fall,
  and become a dream resting under the spring tree.

Start your cultivation early.
Learn to balance your life.
Make your mind and body firm.
This is important.

First weed your mental field,
  allowing not one particle of dust
  to remain in the lens of your mental eye.
When the mind is transparent and subtle,
  the soul becomes supreme.
Then you can use your power as you will.
But do not use it carelessly,
  it is not a plaything.
Accumulate too much wealth
  and it will prove not only burdensome,
  but disastrous.

Gain too high a position,
   and you will find it both dangerous and degrading
   to your true self.
Keep to the roots of your life;
   do not live unconsciously as in a vague dream.

The approach to true happiness
   should not be like a fire
   that dies as quickly as it flares up.
Truly happy people do not clutch at worldly things,
   but appreciate all that comes to them,
   living contentedly with their invisible,
   subtle and immortal natures.
Do not look for happiness
   in the excitement of the sensory world.
Rather, gain an understanding
   of the subtle laws of the universe,
   and happiness shall be yours.
True wisdom can save you.
Move rapidly to board the steady
   spiritual ship of safety.

Chapter 17

The Triune of the Spiritual World

Follow what is indescribable. Ally with what is inexpressible. What is describable is only in the relative sphere. Descriptions also only exist in the relative sphere of language. in the relative sphere of language. What is not expressible is the absolute truth. As stated in Chapter 14 of the *Tao Teh Ching*:

> *"What you try to see,*
> *but evades your vision*
> *you say: Yi!*
> *What you try to hear*
> *but evades your hearing*
> *you say: Shi!*
> *What you try to touch*
> *but evades your hand*
> *you say: Vi!"*

The invisible, the inaudible and the formless are expressed as a triune, but they form an undivided oneness. Because they are of the spiritual realm where intelligence fails to go, they evade all further inquiry. In Taoist terminology this is called "one chi transformed into three Pure Realms."

Yu Ching, or Immaculate Purity, is the name for the unnameable. This realm is for the original immortals such as Yuan Shih.

Shang Ching, or Unblemished Purity, is the name for the imageless. This realm is for the responsive supernatural beings such as Lin-Pau.

Tai Ching, or Great Purity, is the name for the formless. This realm is for the integral ones such as Lan-Chun.

These three Pure Realms maintain the universe totally and are interconnected and integrated in the Subtle Realm.

This Subtle Realm of the Triune is higher and more fundamental than the ordinary Spiritual Realm. It has been the testimony of all achieved Taoists that the Triune is the foundation of the most Subtle Realm. To enter the High Realm is a great achievement. The highest spiritual realm is the Great Pure One, the Tao, the Way and the Law. This is where all spiritual and immortal beings live. Tao is more subtle and original than the spiritual or godly realm. Here, there is no individuality, only various responses to different functions. This is the secret of the great spiritual truth. A god can either be an ordinary human being or one who is highly developed. A highly developed person is achieved and able to dwell in the Divine Immortal Realm. An ordinary human being is an unsuccessful or degraded god who deviated from the Way and therefore dwells in the mortal realm. Surely, this is not the end for people who are unsuccessful in maintaining their spiritual integrity. The last can find their way back to restore their divine nature. then, their achievement is no different from the achieved ones.

In our tradition, only the one who is able to break through the "three in one divided" (the invisible, the inaudible and the untouchable) can conjoin with the real, wonderful, spiritual world.

Chapter 18

Divergence

The Taoist spirit, unobstructed by worldly triviality, is easily misinterpreted as being passive, irresponsible, escapist, lazy, impractical or nonsensical. Such a negative misconception is prevalent among new students. For this reason, readers of Chuang Tzu mistakenly believe that they have learned everything from this great elucidator of Tao. However, the result of their studies indicate otherwise.

An ancient Chinese proverb says, "One assumes he has drawn a tiger, but the tiger turns out to be a dog." Finding such examples is not difficult; understanding the real spirit of a Taoist is not a simple task. The Taoist spirit has no certain form. Thus, how can one hope to make it visible?

A few years ago, a party was given in order to introduce me to some people. I brought a rose with me from my garden for the hostess who was a regular patient of mine. She paid many compliments to this rose of Chinese golden redness. The guest speaker, who was introduced as an expert on oriental philosophy, told the following story:

"Chuang Tzu, one of the great spiritually achieved ones, had a beautiful rose garden of great renown, and every year he would open the garden to the public. Many highly educated people would bring good wine to sip when they came to see the beautiful roses. Reports of this beautiful garden eventually attracted the curiosity of the Emperor, who owned the largest rose garden with the most lovely roses in the kingdom. In order to know whether the acclaimed beauty of Chuang Tzu's garden was true or just a rumor, the Emperor sent a notice to Chuang Tzu announcing when he would arrive to see the specially-cultivated roses. After receiving the king's notice, Chuang Tzu cleared the crowds, closed the garden, and prepared for the important visit.

"When the special day arrived, Chuang Tzu humbly greeted the Emperor at the gate. The Emperor was in high spirits, anticipating his promenade along the garden path. Everywhere, rose bushes filled the garden, but not one of them had even a single rose! The Emperor's consternation grew and grew until it reached a peak. Then suddenly, in the center of the garden, to the Emperor's great surprise, a single rose proudly and brilliantly blossomed. His Majesty's heart was immediately seized by an irresistible fascination with this rose. For a long, long while he was lost in reverie. When his consciousness was restored, he declared this rose the true 'queen' of all roses.

"Dear friends," the speaker said seriously as he went on, "Do you know why the Emperor made this rose the 'queen?' I will tell you. This was actually an ordinary rose, no more beautiful or extraordinary than any other, but before the Emperor's visit Chuang Tzu had cut and removed all the other roses from the garden, leaving only this one in an unexpected place. For that reason, the Emperor believed it to be a truly special rose."

When the speaker had finished his story, I was asked to comment. Having no other choice, I continued the story:

"Ladies and gentlemen, do you know what happened to the Emperor after seeing this wonderful rose? He missed the rose so terribly that he became seriously ill! All his high ministers and generals knew the Emperor's illness was caused by his longing for this special rose, and in desperation, they hastily began to search for a rose of equal beauty. However, since it was wintertime, there were no roses for thousands of miles, and these could not be obtained because of the snow and ice.

"Because their interest was first and foremost to restore the Emperor's health, the high ministers and generals devised a special plan to bring, by way of fast horses, the best roses from the warm lands of the South. People living along this route thought there must be something important happening on their southern border. No one realized that these fast horses were actually carrying just roses.

"The Emperor's health did not improve, however, and in order for him to rest peacefully, he needed to hold a rose in his hand at all times. But when he would awaken, he would discover the lovely rose scattered in petals and become even more ill!

"Since the trouble had developed from Chuang Tzu's rose, the helpless high ministers and generals finally decided to seek his help. Chuang Tzu was a 'clever' master, so he agreed to give his help. It took only a short time for him to take a beautiful rose to the royal court and let the old Emperor - who had not left his ivory sick bed since his illness began - hold it in his hands. No one and nothing had been able to help him feel better until finally he was able to hold one of Chuang Tzu's roses. Now, every time he awoke from his rest, he would see the beautiful rose in all its splendor, safely in his hands.

"The Emperor gradually recovered from his unusual illness and could once again attend to the affairs of state. The people of the entire nation, after learning of his recovery, were thankful and happy.

"Dear friends, are you interested in knowing the secret of the flower that Chuang Tzu took to the Emperor? Let me share it with you. It was an artificial rose, since there were no true roses in the kingdom.

"Confucius, who knew the story of the secret rose, once sighed and sincerely said, 'When worldly people are ill, artificial roses make them feel refreshed. It is not the artificial truth that deserves the blame. It is the artificial truth that makes people lose themselves!'

Chapter 19

Clarify Your Mind

To become one with Tao depends wholly on oneself.
To achieve the level of a shien, a Heavenly being,
    depends solely on your will.
It is possible.

True achievement is obtainable by all
    when they stop clinging selfishly to their desires.
Detach yourself from the irrelevance
    of worldly affairs.
Allow not one piece of dust to stain your true nature,
    and your true essence will reach you clearly
    and shine through all dust.
Then it will be impossible
    for the world's evils and poisons
    to present themselves to you;
    evils that create untold difficulties and problems.

When action is the result of the desires of the mind,
    you perpetuate the painful rounds
    of life, death and rebirth.
You remain unconscious.

Avoid suffering the consequences of your actions
    by ridding your mind of all desire
    for or against anything.
If your desire to achieve is too strong,
    you will disturb your true nature.
Instead of ascending to shiendom,
    you will spiral downward into chaos,
    your subtle nature no longer intact.
Even one impure motive will spawn
    a disturbance in the mind,
    causing you to lose the humility and
    clarity established by Tao.
What you have already achieved,
    you can no longer enjoy.

*Alas, your previous efforts shall all
    have been in vain.*

*Dissolve the poisons of greed and hatred,
    remove yourself from the passions of love,
    and they shall transform into sweet dew,
    cooling and purifying you.*

Chapter 20

The Peace of Tao is Exquisite

Tao is without color or form,
yet from it emerges all wonders of the universe.
Subtly flows the Tao,
deep within the fertile stillness,
hushed within the profound quietude.
It is indeed the Great Reality.

Listen to the silence!

Religions, rich in color and form,
are but creations of the mind of man.
Follow only mental creations
and you will not even scratch the surface.

Watch the invisible!

Trace back to the root of your soul,
found deep within your quiet reflections,
and the ultimate truth unfolds itself naturally.

Feel what you cannot touch!

Self-cultivation will bring you safely
from the shore of beingness
to the vast ocean of non-beingness.
A system, the ferry boat,
is discarded when the destination has been reached.
All man-made religions share the same ignorance;
but through cultivating the root of life,
one may achieve the great awareness.

With the clarity of an illumined mind,
penetrate the illusion of color and form.

Embrace the substance of Nature
and merge with the Origin.

Obstacles will suddenly collapse,
   allowing your inner light to be seen and felt.
In this way, your spiritual flower will surely blossom,
   and you will bear the sweet fruit of immortality.
It is all within your reach,
   but first must come the cultivation,
   the practice, the self-discipline.
This is the true and traditional way
   of becoming one with the Tao.

Unstain and empty the mind;
   thus it will become the fine tool that will unite
   the scattered fragments of yourself into one whole,
   so that what is may become clear.
As the earth gives forth flowers and trees,
   all cultures, civilizations and religions
   are born of the mind.

Magical mind, even more magical when perfectly still!
As a clear and silent pond,
   so should be the mind.
Empty, relaxed, firm, undisturbed,
   thus, and only thus,
   able to know the Truth.
Draw your mind inward to your calm center,
   and all diverse and scattered thoughts will cease.

To follow the impulse of passion and desires
   is to stay trapped in bondage.
Only when you empty the mind
   can you verify and experience
   the wonders of the eternal realms.
But attach yourself, even to this empty mind,
   and you remain yet outside the Tao.

Cling neither to emptiness nor to concepts;
   this is the proper way to take care of your mind.
Guard and cleanse the gates of the six senses
   so that you will not be deceived by them.

The calculating mind cannot be trusted,
because hidden in its roots
are the distorted thoughts and feelings
of pain, bitterness and sadness.
Boldly swing the sword of wisdom,
and cut yourself free from the shell of illusion
that binds and confines you.
Beware of being tricked by vanity.
Love, fame, profit and high position
are the golden harvest moon
bobbing on the surface of a lake.

Do not let the world disturb you.
Maintain unshakable quiescence
and enjoy the exquisite peace.
In your experience of this aspect of true freedom,
understand the real Void is not void at all!
Through unrelenting self-discipline,
the hidden truths of the universe will unfold.

Chapter 21

Cross the Mist of the Sea
To the Shore of Crystal Clarity

When cultivating the Tao,
    rid yourself of illusion.
Cast off the limitations
    of the body and mind.
Do not get caught in conflicts
    between yourself and the world.
Only in this way,
    can whole and complete freedom be found.

Dissolve the difference
    between yourself and objects;
    no longer be bothered by color or form.
Remove the dirty clothing
    of your pain and bitterness,
    and your true nature will instantly appear.

Though the Way is boundless,
    persistence will deliver you
    to the distant shore.
Continue on!
Do not stop before reaching your destination.
Succeed!
And experience the indescribable happiness of purity.

Work night and day in your efforts.
Courageously face all tests and trials.
Here and now surpass all distinctions
    between yourself and Heaven.
Then, in one final step,
    you will be able to cross
    the bitter sea to the crystal shore.
Never, from beginning to end,
    lose sight of this goal.

When your cultivation is finally complete,
   full will be the merits and virtues.

Always remember,
   that in the nothingness of mind,
   the seed of a whole being can be found.

Chapter 22

The Light in Self-Cultivation

The goal of self-cultivation is to return to one's natural state of purity. Through cultivating the self, one can see one's true nature by the light of one's own unfolding intelligence. Turn inward and examine every part of yourself. Follow what is right and eliminate what is wrong. All things depend upon the harmony of one's will and the will of the subtle realm. Do the best you can, and leave the result to the subtle realm.

Maintain strict discipline under any circumstances. Relinquish worldly ambitions and abandon worldly cares. Do not live a shallow life. To be awakened to the path and still adhere to your old, inferior habits is disastrous.

Still the mind and its passionate nature. Learn to say "no" to friends and especially "no" to yourself. You will receive strength from conquering an overwhelming desire. It might seem easier to straighten the winding rivers and mountains than to alter the disposition of a rigid mind. Regulate your temper and cultivate your heart.

With undaunted determination, one can become a true immortal being if one has worked on his self-cultivation and transformed himself to a more subtle level of pure existence in body, mind and spirit. Human beings have the potential to evolve to this higher form of life.

Chapter 23

Progress Towards the Eternal Infinitude

Do not mistake false illusions for reality.
Cast your light within
  to look at your own reflection.
Worldly affairs are but empty dreams.
All the wealth in the world
  is not worth any more
  than one strand of your hair.

The place where a being of wholeness comes from
  can only be seen with a mind that is pure.
Rid yourself of all thoughts and mental activity,
  and see the origin of goodness.

Retreat, pull back, confine yourself,
  keep still your mind,
  and the outer world's temptations
  will melt like ice.
Control each subtle square inch of your mind.
Eliminate mental confusions;
  many there are.
Preferences and other worldly dyes
  stain your body and mind.
Though it is difficult at first to discipline yourself,
  good habits, once formed, come naturally.
You will be rewarded for your discipline,
  truly and completely.
The happiness which will come to surround you
  is unspeakable.

Once you no longer follow
  the moving stream of your consciousness,
  the rounds of life and death will be broken.
Take leave of false phenomena.
Surpass all form and you will discover
  that reality is the subtle nature
  that is everywhere, yet nowhere to be seen.

Follow reality like a road
   by cultivating your trueness.
Leave the limited concepts of form,
   and so progress toward the invisible,
   eternal infinitude.
The Sacred Method is simple;
   the seed needs only to be molded.

Chapter 24

Self-Integration

Becoming spiritually integrated means giving up the false beliefs of a conceptual world and keeping one's own true nature deeply connected with the universe. The following guidelines will help you to self-revival or self-integration:

1. Unify the mind and body so there is no separation. This means to eliminate internal conflict, such as physical interest and the extreme religious interest.

2. Concentrate on inner vitality and on becoming pliant like a baby. This means to restore the natural condition of one's life being in order to nurture the essence of life.

3. Purify the inner vision in order to reach immaculate accuracy. This means to remove religious blockage which harms your reaching for the unnameable natural spiritual truth.

4. Love all people and govern the country with serviceable virtue instead of resorting to the worldly approach of force.

5. Be receptive when the Heavenly door opens and closes. This brings forth the subtle changes that appear in the physical world. This means apply no assertiveness in one's life when one faces the merely external changes. This means little to your inner essence of life, which you should embrace all the time.

6. Be crystal clear with an innocent mind.

7. Keep your mind and life unoccupied in order to live with the reality of each new moment.

Chapter 25

The Non-Glaring Light of True Wisdom

First know that without challenges,
*   one cannot become a sage.*
Without undaunted determination
*   to walk the right way,*
*   one cannot attain true wisdom.*
One should give up all kinds of strange paths
*   and return to the plain truth of nature.*

Flowery words are not to be trusted,
*   for the truth is simple and unadorned.*
Never tire of studying life.
Ceaselessly gather your chi
*   and keep it whole.*
Essence, chi and spirit
*   are the three jewels of life.*
When chi is high,
*   one can triumph over all negativity;*
When it is low,
*   one will be prey to it.*

Only with developed spiritual eyes
*   can one discern the marrow of wisdom*
*   in oneself and others.*
One must meditate and cultivate oneself for many years
*   before experiencing the high mysterious intelligence.*
Self-cultivation ennobles one's personality.
Keep your senses in perfect quietude.
Do not contend with anyone.
The struggle for supremacy
*   destroys one's high spiritual quality.*
When living with others, keep peace.
When living alone, beware of negative thoughts.
Never commit faults because you consider them small.

When nature sends calamities,
*   it is still possible to escape;*

When one creates the calamity oneself,
  one has to suffer the consequences.
Prevent disease by taking good care
  of yourself when healthy.
Do not treat anyone or anything with indifference.
Your behavior has serious consequences
  to your health, your family and your very life.
One who is noble in spirit,
  does not covet what others take pride in:
  their things, their occupations, or their interests.
If you see something you like,
  restrain the desire;
  follow what is in your own nature.

Chapter 26

Non-Possession

The body you are using does not belong to you.
It is the result of the interaction of the chi
* of light spirit and heavy physics.*
One's spiritual nature is handed down
* from the divine Subtle Realm.*
Why is it that we lead our lives
* in selfish delusions?*
In the midst of this material world,
* the deluded mind exhausts itself*
* by endlessly chasing ups, downs*
* gains and losses.*
The moment the servant of death knocks at the door,
* it is too late to regret*
* that one's life has been passed in vain.*

In earlier days, we were enlightened
* by breaking through our illusions*
* with the help of our masters.*
Today we must strengthen our life source anew
* from the root.*

We borrow this pure, clean, divine essence
* from Heaven.*
It should be returned without contamination.
Do not stain it with dirt and filth
* or soil it with flaws and corruption.*
It is an allowance from the divine Heaven
* and is handed to us for positive use.*
Only fools try to possess it.

We come from nothingness and possess nothing.
Our only wish is to become eternally one
* with the harmonizing entirety.*

Henceforth, we are awakened
* from the midst of our dream.*

After awakening, there is nothing
    which can be recognized as the ego.
Deeply, from our hearts, we offer our lives
    in dedication to the reintegration
    of Heaven, Earth and Humankind -
    the spiritual integration of the universe.
Every worldly deed, whether for self or for others,
    is dedicated as an offering to the Subtle Origin.
We offer our worship as a direct response,
    with absolute sincerity to the Subtle Divine Realm.
All the shiens in Heaven are our witnesses.
Our resolution is as vast and deep
    as the mountains and oceans.
Thus, our hearts are rooted firmly.
We never evade our responsibility out of greed,
    because the net of Heavenly laws
    cannot be escaped.
We always maintain Heaven's ever-permeating,
    righteous chi.

Chapter 27

Internal Power is Far Greater Than External Force

Gently gather your energy,
*   and quiet your wandering mind.*
Carefully filter your desires
*   to protect your vitality.*
You will radiate with an auspicious light.
All of Heaven and its deities,
*   all of Earth and its people,*
*   respect this kind of light.*
The power you acquire and are able to use,
*   is released by your tranquil mind.*

Internal powers are far greater than external strength.
With calmness comes wisdom.
The clouds part, the moon becomes bright,
*   and all directions shine with the light.*
Surpass the sacred method with the sacred method,
*   then no more method will there be.*
You and the method become one.
The deepest, most wondrous silence
*   comes by forgetting the active.*
This is the level where you become the great king
*   of the sacred method of liberation,*
*   at last able to enjoy its fruit.*

True happiness can come only from
*   rightful discipline and patience.*
Use your courageous mental powers
*   to withstand fear and anxiety.*
The existence or non-existence of your physical body
*   is not cause for worry.*
True spirit has no worry or fear.
This is how to be a developed being.

Chapter 28

The Secret of Achievement Lies In the Persistence of a Clear Mind

It is not difficult to cultivate and understand reality.
The secret of achievement lies in
the persistence of a pure mind.
Once you begin the sacred method,
follow it only.
The constancy of your efforts
will cause the wisdom of your soul to shine through.
Following different approaches
disperses your energies,
creates chaos and delays in your achievement.
Self-cultivation creates a firm, calm power.
Through it, your efforts and hopes
to transcend the mediocre will be realized.
Stay with one method from beginning to end.
Avoid the temptation to change paths.
Honesty and sincerity are connected;
each influences the other.
With them, all positive, subtle energy
protects you.
Your subtle body has form,
but is not limited to it.
True wisdom is quiet,
independent and fragrant.
Persevere in connecting with the universal light.
Through it you will achieve
the fullness and brightness
of your own nature.
You yourself can experience and verify
the greatness of eternal truth,
and thereby voyage safely
across the boundless spiritual ocean.
Know that your own intelligence can create blindness.
Be diligent in changing night into day.
It is easiest to progress with self-cultivation
in a quiet, dark and separate room.

> *The grace from all the subtle worlds will come to you*
> *and make you the wise, firm seed*
> *of a Heavenly whole being,*
> *a shien, a most beautifully developed one.*

Chapter 29

Water: The Example of Natural Virtue

The following are eight natural ways of virtue in which people of integral virtue can learn from Water:

1. Be content with a "low" position. Like Water, by remaining low, one may be safe and free from competition.[2]

2. Remain profound. A profound mind is as quiet as the deep ocean. Therefore, it is undisturbed by the waves on the surface.

3. Give generously. Water constantly gives without asking to be repaid.

4. Speak faithfully. The flow of Water always faithfully goes toward the sea.

5. Govern gently. Although water moves with gentleness, it can overcome even the hardest obstacle under Heaven.

6. Work capably and adaptably. Water can fit what is square or what is round. It keeps its true nature in any containment or circumstance.

7. Take action opportunely. Water freezes in Winter and melts in Spring. Its inflexibility in the Winter is

---

[2]This implies that humans like to be in "high" positions rather than "low" ones. This becomes a source of conflict for many. Those on a high tight rope always need to look for balance points by using a parasol or pole. For the one who walks on the ground, a fully opened parasol or pole is a great nuisance.

like death. Its softness in the Spring generates new life.

8. Never fight. Water does not fight for itself, thus it is beyond blame.

Chapter 30

Cultivating the Mind

The mind and the heart represent the Fire energy in our
bodies. Only when they are harmonized with the body
which represent the Water energy, can one achieve the
correct goal of fundamental cultivation: good health.

Keep the mind clear;
this is more valuable than knowledge.
Inquire into the properties of things
and penetrate to their essence.
Do not be excessive in anything,
not even in joy.
When joy is overabundant,
it must turn to become its opposite,
and sorrow will overcome you.
When pleasure is carried through to its highest degree,
it will bring about sadness.

Nourish the body with calmness.
Nourish the heart by giving to others.
The more you give to others,
the more you will abound.

When righteousness lives in the eyes,
they become bright.
If you keep negativity in your mind,
calamities are sure to come.
If you keep your mind open and receptive,
it can absorb knowledge quickly.
The mind of a superior being
is imbued with righteousness.
When the mind approaches true happiness,
it becomes intelligent.
Keep the mind unoccupied, receptive and loose.
Do not hold on to anything, good or bad.
Know that everything is in constant change.
Nothing is static.

Be thorough in your actions,
    but keep your mind empty.
Through creative non-action,
    one can extend the clarity of one's mind
    and the innocence of one's pristine spirit
    to embrace the eternal Tao.
When the mind betrays the pristine spirit,
    it becomes a monkey, jumping from here to there.
It becomes lewd, compromising and boasting.
Where is the beauty of your tranquil mind?
Cut deep into the core of your problems.
Cut out all falseness and conditioned ideas.
He who conquers his mind is really great.
Disarm it, conquer its willfulness.

Know that your mind is like spring water.
Its purity will emerge from the depths of your soul.
United with the spirit, it will express true beauty.
You will be earnest, contented,
    unconcerned with daily life, joyous.
You will be a useful vessel to assist others
    on the road to Tao.

We have to nourish the heart.
When we have little desire, the heart is content.
When we hold on to nothing,
    the heart becomes carefree.
Soon the heart is as a leaf
    trembling in an imperceptible breeze,
    as light as the dust on a butterfly's wings.

Closing the senses is perceiving life.
Perceiving no thing,
    be perceptive to the utmost depth.
Penetrate the impenetrable.
Perceive the imperceivable.
Such a small beginning
    to the wide, unlimited ascension.

Chapter 31

Love

The mutual response of two young hearts presents the picture of love. This is illustrated by ☵ a young girl, and ☶a young boy, and the mutual attraction shared between them.

When I was young, I focused more on my spiritual achievement than on experiences of love. After studying the important teachings of the three main cultural traditions - Taoism, Confucianism and Buddhism - I harmonized and expressed all three with the following words:

> *"Confucianism is my garment,*
> *Buddhism is my cane and*
> *Taoism is my sandal."*

(For more information regarding this saying, refer to the commentary for Hexagram #45.) My young, proud mind seemed to be satisfied with this combination. However, one day I discovered that someone had added some new, handwritten words to each line of my writing on the wall of my study. These lines now said:

> "Confucianism is my garment,
> *- it is too short for you!*
> Buddhism is my cane,
> *- it is too weak to support you!*
> and Taoism is my sandal
> *- it has been worn out long ago!"*

My first response to this discovery was outrage. I thought it must be my younger brother or elder sister making fun of me, but since it did not seem to be an ordinary joke, I immediately corrected my judgment. The person who wrote these lines had to have a vision higher than, or equal to, mine. I felt puzzled. Who could have done this? Since the handwriting was not much better than mine, it could not be the work of a dignified adult. Also, this happened to be my personal study upstairs. I was the only one who used most of the upstairs rooms, except for the one used as the family shrine. After making many inquiries of my family, I discovered that some of my sister's girlfriends had visited us. One of them had been in our family shrine for a short while. She was the only daughter of one of my father's friends. She had to be the one who did this. She was famous for being the most beautiful girl in our town. She was also well-educated and a lover of literature.

Though I had never paid attention to her before, I decided I must pay her a visit. I thought of the ancient one's saying: "Three people are walking together; one of them must have something I can learn." I dressed myself neatly and directly went to see her.

She received me in the small hall of their garden. After our greeting, I politely and straightforwardly requested an explanation of the addition I was certain she had made on my study wall. She flushed and suggested that if I would call on her for ten days she would then give me her explanation. I agreed to this as my respectful lesson. Thus, every afternoon I went to her house. We read some good, ancient poetry, played Chinese chess and did some gardening. Our friendship developed more with each day. When she tenderly touched the back of my hand, I felt that something had struck me, yet I liked it. Her eyes were the most beautiful poem I had ever read. The sweetness of her delicate smell intoxicated me. Her smile engulfed me.

Before long, however, a difficulty surfaced in our budding romance. It appeared that she was especially attached to a novel entitled *The Red Chamber*. I could never agree with her belief that *The Red Chamber* held the truth of life and, likewise, she could never agree with my Kung Fu practice.

When we reached the end of our ten-day period together, I again requested her explanation of the lines she had written on my wall. She asked for my palm, upon which she wrote a Chinese character with her gentle, slim finger. The Chinese word struck me in the same way I was struck by her finger, moving lightly over my palm. It was the character for the word "love" or, more appropriately in this case, "affection."

Now I was even more bewildered than before. I could not refrain from asking her what connection could possibly exist between the love of which she spoke and her addition to my writing. At first she hesitated. Then finally, with apparent difficulty, she said, "You like to think much of Confucianism, Buddhism and Taoism, but without the word 'love' nothing has any meaning in life. Have you ever thought of that?"

This was a real question for me. Since I had never experienced love, I had never truly pondered this question. I answered frankly, "I do not know yet. How do you know?"

"From *The Red Chamber*," she answered.

I frowned. I had read the book and did not like it. When I told her that, she responded, "What is wrong with a girl and a boy falling in love as described in that book?"

"I don't know. It seems like too much trouble to become involved in such complicated love," I replied.

"Well, it seems to me like Confucianism, Buddhism and Taoism give you even more trouble with all kinds of study and discipline," she argued.

"I haven't thought about that. However, you have given me your explanation. I shall now go home to discover, through my own cultivation, the true significance of that word."

Though it was time to say good-bye, her eyes kept staring into mine and I felt their warmth flow into my body. Gradually, her eyes became moistened, tears falling from them like a string of pearls. I did not know how to help her. After a long while with her handkerchief to her face, she said, "You are always contemptuous toward me and the other girls. You will not come to see me again."

"I don't know. I'll think about it," I replied.

"It will be too late to see me if you only think about it. I shall die only for love, like Blue Jade (the main female character in *The Red Chamber*). Can you understand?" she asked.

"I shall go home and study this book that you like so much."

She offered, "I would like for you to have my copy since it is the best version." She went into her inner room to get the copy of her "holy book" and gave it to me. I took the book and left.

Though we had several versions of *The Red Chamber* in our house, I had never been able to read through any one of them in its entirety. The main story described the life of Precious Jade, a young man of a noble and wealthy family. Although his youth was spent in an elegant garden with many beautiful girls as his companions, he fell in love only with Blue Jade. However, his family arranged for him to marry a girl for whom he had no love. Soon afterward, Blue Jade died from her disappointment in love. Precious Jade's family also suffered decline. Precious Jade himself discovered that his entire life was an empty dream and thus he decided to leave the dusty world to become a Buddhist monk.

Though this book was a good work of literature, the love it described was narrow. I could not recognize any high truth with which the author could illuminate human life. However, since I liked to have her be one of my friends, and because I still felt difficulty with the question of love, I turned to my mother for help.

My mother told me, "An ancient sage once said, 'Even a developed one feels trouble communicating with women and children.' Problems are created when people of different levels of development come together. Therefore, spiritual development sometimes makes it more difficult to be with ordinary people. If this shortcoming of a developed person is not moderated, it can bring extreme isolation to him. This would not be a beneficial direction for anyone to go in, unless it is done so intentionally, with a positive purpose for some special cultivation.

"Love is an important matter in life. Nobody can ignore it. In general, as you already know, love can be classified into two different categories: broad love and narrow love. Broad love is humanistic, and all the ancient sages were recognized for their broad love. Confucius (551-416 B.C.) and Mencius (372-298 B.C.) exalted humanistic love. Mo Tzu (501-479 B.C.) exalted universal love and made himself as a model to realize it. He led a life of absolute self-abnegation. He exerted himself to the fullest extent of his life by working for the peace of humanity. Lao Tzu valued natural impartial love as the highest level. Sakyamuni exalted compassion and equal love. In general, humanistic love is developed, peaceful, impersonal and dispassionate love. This is what human nature was born with and what human beings should continue to cultivate. Also, in general, narrow love can only be practiced between two people, like a boy and a girl, a man and a woman, a husband and wife, or among a group of people like a family, a circle of friends, a religious fellowship, a society, a nation or a race.

"The practice of narrow love is usually passionate. Passion means emotion. Passion is what makes love narrow. Passionate love can be a good experience during one's youth, but passion needs to be well-guided and controlled. Although the emotional experience of narrow love can be beautiful, it can also be harmful. Broad, humanistic or natural love, however, can be enjoyed throughout this life and all lives. Whether love is humanistic or passionate, it should always be guided by the principle of balance. If one loses balance in the name of love, then that way of loving is unhealthy.

"All people are born with passion, yet different patterns of passion give people different temperaments. One's temperament is influenced by all the stages of one's pre-natal and postnatal life. Parents must take the great responsibility to smooth their own temperaments when raising children in their pre-natal and post-natal stages. An individual must also take responsibility to cultivate himself and regulate his own temperament when a certain level of growth is reached, or as the saying goes, 'An adult must take responsibility for his own ugly face.'

"Now we come to the matter of adjusting one's personal temperament. One's temperament is like one's dog: one needs to put a muzzle and leash on it when taking it in public. Surely achievement comes when one has cast off one's 'dog' nature which is molded by the environment.

"Passion is natural. It is something we are born with, but the way we express our passion is a matter of our environment. We develop that expression ourselves, thus it is controllable and reformable.

"Passion is like water. Water is always water, but in its different phases, the speed and shape of its flow vary greatly. It can be a swift current, a big flood or a torrent. It can be slow moving, or stagnant and motionless. It can also be a rising or ebbing tide, overflowing or draining a stream, lake, ravine, river or ocean. When water meets heat, it becomes vapor; when it meets cold, it becomes ice. Dew, rain, hail, fog, frost, ice, snow and so forth, all come from water. The water always remains the same - it is the environment which causes its different characteristics. Passion is like that.

"Passion is only a part of the whole human mental being, however. There is still the higher sphere of the mind which needs to be cultivated and developed so that one can have good control over the passion of the lower sphere of the mind. A raft riding the torrents cannot carry many people. Danger may be lurking anywhere along the path. Though one may enjoy the excitement of riding a raft in the torrents, this is not a normal, everyday practice. If one's passion is like a torrent, then one's life is like a raft. How dangerous that is! How long can the enjoyment of such excitement last? Is it worth exhausting one's life? This seems to be a poor model of normal, healthy passion.

"Love is a beautiful passion; however, when emotional force or possessiveness is attached to what one loves, the sublime state of pure love is degraded or damaged. Surely, a spiritually developed person can still feel personal love, but it is unattached and unoccupying love. This is the fine quality of true spiritual love. The nature of spiritual love is subtle. One can unceasingly appreciate beauty without creating the troubles which accompany its ownership. Therefore, a full life of appreciation can be lived without carrying the weight of worldly burdens.

"Out of one's humanistic love comes the courage to accept responsibility for the world. This is certainly not a rigid practice. Most ancient Taoists, if not living in the high mountains married to the beauty of nature, would travel around the world like a white cloud flying across the sky. Nothing could restrict them.

"The particular practice of love in our family is to reach the level of the ancient Taoists. We follow the external patterns of secular life, but within this everyday life we fulfill the broadness of spiritually. In other words, we use the roughness of the world and the difficulties of practical life as the friction that creates our spiritual sparks. This is what people call enlightenment or inspiration. Though enlightenment and inspiration are only momentary experiences, they can mark where one has reached. Furthermore, the endurance of life, which is built from the difficulties of worldly life, is our actual realization of universal, impartial love. The refinement of one's passions and emotions becomes an important aspect in this realization.

"Some people cannot see with their partial vision that the truth is total. They think there can be no existence of individual happiness in the practice of humanistic love, but the real truth is that individual happiness exists only in the happiness of its completeness. Can one have happiness when the entire world suffers from a flood? One can only fulfill one's own life through the harmonious fulfillment of all lives. That is why, in our family, we live for ourselves as well as for the entire world, with a clear spiritual direction."

Then my mother continued, "In the narrow sense of a family, your father is our life-maker. I am the home-maker and also a life-maker. We are all makers of a common life. We fulfill our individual duty and also assist the fulfillment of each other's duty. I am eighteen years younger than your father. I respect and love him and he has much tolerance and understanding toward me. Actually, he treats the entire world this same way, but I am the one who has the blessing to live with him. Furthermore, your father is a man of spiritual development, thus our love is mainly spiritual rather than physical. Being spiritually linked is the source of our happiness.

"If love is true, the experience of love and deep joy occur in the same moment. It is not joyful to reminisce about a particular moment of love in the past. The enlightenment of love exists in each moment. There is no search that can find love, nor any occasion that can create love. You know love when your heart is open. The music is silent, but its harmony pervades your entire being. In that moment there is no separation.

"Love is the golden light of the sun rising within your being. It is the rose which has just opened its eyes. It is the freshness of dew or the caress of a wave on the shore - all within you.

"But the dawn becomes noon and finally evening. The early morning dew evaporates. The rose reaches its fullness and its petals fall. A wave reaches its crest and returns to the sea. Then, does love also die? If the love within us is living, does it also die when it reaches its fullness? Can one hold that certain moment of the sun's first appearance on the horizon? Can one make love endure? At what point does the joy of love's presence become the need for its possession? When one fears it will go away or die is when the need for its possession arises. At this point love becomes contaminated with emotion and need, and its original harmony changes to dissonance. Love then reverts to the realm of duality, and the presence of Tao within our hearts is missed.

"Love can be fulfilled without becoming trapped in the web of emotional needs. We can learn from the virtue of a well which exists for all to take from. Its spring never runs dry. When our inner treasure is inexhaustible, we can provide limitless love and still remain independent and non-possessing.

"In our tradition, we can enjoy the sunrise within us every moment. Our love is as free as the blowing wind and as enduring as a flowing river. Since we continually renew ourselves, we do not fear losing love. Our cultivation becomes our lover, for our love is Tao. Thus, love never withers, for it is continually refreshed.

"When the time comes that you feel love for someone, be gentle. Love has a delicate nature. Never be rough with it or it will be completely destroyed. Always distinguish the difference between love and desire. Love gives pleasure; desire creates pressure. Desire, loneliness, tension and disappointment can all deteriorate the delicate nature of true love. To love is to be gentle. Tender love is truly beneficial in any circumstance. If love is not given gently, it becomes stormy. Stormy love, like stormy weather, can never last long. Generally this kind of love comes out of an imbalance in one's personality or from the pressures of an unhealthy environment.

"Young people may say tender love is weak love, but this is not true. Motherly love is tender love. An eagle soars in the sky and finds its prey among a group of small chickens searching for food in a meadow. It quickly dives to the ground, but before it can extend its sharp claws to capture its prey, the weak old mother hen has already spread her wings and gathered all her chicks under them. She puts herself, face to face, in confrontation with the aggressor. Love can give birth to courage and courage can subdue the strong. You have witnessed this great scene many times in our country life.

"I always tell your sisters that a woman should never become emotionally competitive with her man. A man does not like to have another 'manly' person in his private life. I also tell your sisters to be responsible in family life, but not bossy. A man may have enough bosses in his life outside the family. A woman must earn love and respect from a man by being feminine and by being faithful, not by fighting or competing.

"You feel troubled about correctly responding to the love that comes from this good girl. You can love her if it is your true response. This might be the first time you sail the oceans of love. However, there is nothing to be afraid of. When the current becomes rough, keep yourself centered as usual, and get complete control of your ship. As far as I can see, this girl is not a torrential type of girl. She is more like the beautiful flow of a brooklet; the poetic feeling of her presence can calmly be absorbed.

"However, do not develop your young spiritual love into sentimental love. The love of Precious Jade and Blue Jade is not a good example of pure love. It is not healthy to imitate it. Healthy love bears the fruit of deep rejoicing; nothing can alter it and nothing can be exchanged for it. The beauty of sentimental love can earn wide appreciation on a literary level. However, if it occurs in practical life, it must be the result of an emotional imbalance or feelings of insecurity. Above all, such imaginary love lasts for only a short time. Her imitation of Blue Jade should not be encouraged by you through helping her all day to prepare a funeral for the fallen flower petals and then helping her bury them while singing the funeral hymn. I heard she has been doing this already for years. This is a silly matter, and it is ominous to accept the suggested destiny of Blue Jade in *The Red Chamber*.

"The challenge she makes on your young spiritual authority will surely benefit you. Remember, never be bothered about those who speak or write better than you. Always be mindful of achieving your own transpiercing vision of reality. She has not developed higher than you. Her motivation could be need for love rather than spiritual communication. Now, restore your inner balance and give her an answer."

The same day, I wrote my answer to her and returned her copy of *The Red Chamber*. The following is what I wrote:

> *"Confucianism is my garment,*
>   *- it is too short for me.*
> *Buddhism is my cane,*
>   *- it is too weak to support me.*
> *Now I become a worshipper of* The Red Chamber.
>
> *I am going to help Precious Jade secularize*
>   *from his tedious life as a monk.*
> *I am going to revive his Blue Jade*
>   *with my Taoist Magic."*

Chapter 32

The Wholeness of Our Life Spirit

The natural principle expressed by one who is whole
is the enduring spiritual energy of life.

In the midst of all changes,
*   remain undisturbed.*
Whether the days are good or bad,
*   whether dealing with virtuous or unvirtuous ones,*
*   do not leave the wholeness of your spirit.*

What is the enduring spirit of life?
It is the same as the spirit of the universe,
*   which is governed by constancy,*
*   regularity and spontaneity.*
With its eternal virtuous nature,
*   it nourishes and cares for all things.*

Virtue is the inherent nature of life.
That which is inherent in the nature of life
*   is inherent in your own nature.*
In order to restore the enduring spirit,
*   we have to practice its subtleties.*
From nature,
*   people are endowed with discernment.*
They can actively change the rigidity of their mind,
*   dissolving destructive tendencies*
*   and false images by means of*
*   practicing constant virtue.*
Thus, they arrive at the delicateness
*   of their spirit,*
*   which is creative, useful*
*   and beneficial to all.*

Chapter 33

Pure Heart and Mind

To achieve spiritual integrity in Tao,
  the emphasis belongs not on worldly affairs,
  but on keeping the mind still.
This you know.
As worldly interest lessens,
  interest in Tao increases.
As your mind becomes empty,
  the Tao fills your being.
With heart and mind pure,
  negativity and evil fail to lure.
Only by observing and correcting yourself
  can you eliminate the pain and torture
  you allow to occur.
Meaningless, deceptive,
  and vastly exaggerated
  are all worldly pleasure and pain:
  illusions we ourselves form.
What confusion and bewilderment they cause!
How they keep us from being free!
See through these obstacles
  and all hindrances in your path will disappear.
That these things are not a hindrance,
  enlightened people know.
Progress first by one step and then another:
  methodically, carefully,
  break through your confusion.

Silence is the ideal.
Merely talking about self-cultivation
  lacks any real benefit.
Allow Tao to penetrate
  and it will expand,
  filling your body and being.
Your way of life will be
  naturally smooth and straight.

Wholehearted you will be,
   with strong, protective power,
   forsaking the bitterness of life,
   content within yourself.
Because all lives are just like yours,
   all things are one body within you.
This secret is clear,
   and with this comes the confirmation
   that you have the seed of a whole being.

Chapter 34

Premature Enlightenment

The following is an anecdote of an early spiritual experience I had before I obtained instruction on the true mind from my father. It helps illustrate hexagram 34, Ta Chuang, ☲ "being overly strong."

In my home town there were several good libraries, as well as a number of good book stores. One day, after having exhausted all the private libraries in our town, I ventured to the city in order to satiate my young desire for more knowledge, especially in matters of history and of spirit. It was a walk of fifteen li (approximately five miles) one way, so I carried my lunch with me in a package of lotus leaves.

Within this neighboring city, there was a Buddhist library in which I often found myself. It was set in a Buddhist temple and was especially nice and quiet for reading, except on days when there was a ceremony. During this period of my youth, I was a fervent reader of Buddhism and was permitted to read from any book on the tall, wooden bookshelves in this temple. Because my reading speed was fast, I needed only to stand in front of those tall book shelves to finish reading several books. At one time while I was standing there before I moved myself to another section of shelves. To my annoyance, after a few days a monk began appearing who dusted the room in such a manner that I always had to move to make way for him. After this had occurred many times, I discovered that the monk was doing this intentionally. I finally said to him, "Please do not create dust while I am reading. It disturbs my eyes."

"Pardon me, but is it the 'dust' on the shelves which disturbs your eyes, or is it my work?" the monk queried.

This question made me aware of his implicit challenge, and I answered, "I came here to discover what the 'dust' is which covers the eyes of all good Chinese people and, to my surprise, I find one here who buries himself in dust as his profession."

The monk responded, "Well, well, I mistook a tiger for a dog. Come into my room. Let us share a cup of tea."

I accepted the invitation and went with him to his room. After putting the tea set on the table, he said, "If you answer this question correctly, I will serve you tea." I agreed, and he asked, "What is Buddha Dharma?"

"Have a cup of tea!" I replied. He poured the tea into my cup. I started to pick up the cup, ready to drink, when suddenly he seized my hand and said, "Wait a moment, you have not asked me yet."

"All right, what is Buddha Dharma?" I asked.

"Have a cup of tea, sir," was his reply.

We both laughed. After a sip of tea, he asked again, "What is the spectrum of achievement of Buddha?" I replied:

> *"Like wayfarer worn,*
> *up homeward hill paths,*
> *straining for scenes that*
> *anxious eyes may rest.*
> *Pavilion lone,*
> *its loved one gone.*
> *Vain kept the swallows their nest."*

Then it was my turn to ask him, and he said, "Here, within me, I leave no room for the old Buddha. Therefore, there is absolutely no Buddha shadow within me. What I have is my own spectrum of achievement, which may be worthy for entertaining my young guest. I make this offering; listen!"

He paused and then continued:

> *"Moon gleamed like frost.*
> *Breeze free like fluid,*
> *pure world without bound.*
> *Up crooked reaches fish leaped,*
> *on lotus leaves dew distilled,*
> *quietude without sound.*
> *Lo, a third time*
> *of time-telling drum in the late night.*
> *Loud dropped a leaf -*
> *broke me from dreams profound.*

> *Night stretched dim.*
> *The return missed,*
>   *at dawn I paced the garden round."*

I could appreciate his answer and he also appreciated mine, thus through this meeting we became good friends.

At this time I was around seventeen. During that summer, I started to "preach" to my friends and, as my convictions were strong, I felt there was no one more superior than I. I would use the corridor of our house at the side of the canal as the gathering place where people could enjoy the breeze while they listened to my talk. Usually when I spoke I would be giving my doctrine of self-authority to the neighborhood kids. This was what I usually said:

"Believe nobody. There is no God, there is no Buddha, there is no authority but yourself as the real authority of your life. In other words, I am the true God. I am the true Buddha. I am the true Way. I am the authority of my life. Therefore, there is no need to worship any sort of divinity. Do not go to the temple; do not go to the church; do not make pilgrimages to any place. Your holy land is within yourself. Most important, never recognize any authority. Deny all sages, and deny what our ancestors said. Your teacher, parents, grandparents and all other people are not the authorities of your life; it is no one but you."

I earned many new friends by using my young usurping "religious" ideas. Some families were troubled by my influence. My brother said I was mad. Some of the parents wished that my father would stop me. My father told them, "All great world teachings are premature or half-mature. False teachers find many followers; true teachers have few. False teachings make people strong and rigid; true teachings make people gentle and pliant. All teachings are for the purpose of growth. Should we obstruct the growth of our children?"

One day at noon, during our main meal, my mother sent my brother several times to get me. Instead of returning with him, I kept talking and talking, becoming wilder and wilder. When I finished, I walked into the dining room. To my amazement, there was no food on the table.

I walked into the kitchen; there was no food there. I walked to the other part of the house; no one was around, except for my father. Being busy as usual with his patients, we had no chance to exchange any words. I went upstairs to my own room, since I wished to rest. My hunger, however, kept me restless and there was a constant noise in my belly. I rushed down to look again for my mother and the rest of the family. This time my father told me they were all out visiting friends and he was not sure when they would return. He said my mother had suggested it might be a good idea for me to fast for the rest of the day, so I returned to my room. From upstairs, I could look out to the front and see the canal, or from the back I could view the luxurious green fields reaching to the mountains. Here I could study, meditate, practice Kung Fu and do other spiritual activities. This was a great gift of my youth, where I could quietly lay the foundation for my future spiritual development without disturbance.

But this particular occasion was not easy for me. Because I held my doctrine, "Everybody is the authority of his own life," I thought surely my mother or sisters should not have to cook for me all the time. Furthermore, since I am the authority of my own life, why bother to eat? During the first part of this long summer afternoon, I was determined to live by my convictions. Then as evening came, I noticed the setting sun was not as delightful as usual. The evening breeze which comes with the twilight of the stars was not as cool and pleasant as usual either. This night also seemed much longer than usual. However, being the authority of my own life, I thought I could at least make it useful for sleeping. Let me tell you, when your stomach feels full it is easy to sleep, but when your stomach is empty it is not so easy to reach calmness. Nevertheless, I went to sleep but suddenly awakened after midnight.

In the early hours of the morning, I began to examine my great spiritual system obtained from my own enlightenment. Reflecting on the condition of the empty stomach, the fresh brain, the music of the crickets and frogs below and the subtle light in the sky, it was easy for me to rediscover that no life could forget its physiological base and that no individual could claim authority over life. No food could starve a person. No air could suffocate a person. And on and on, until my self-authority became more and more thinly supported and, finally, I fell into a sound sleep.

When the morning sun awakened me with its golden smile, it was already thirty rules high (forty to fifty degrees). I washed myself and prepared for the great spiritual meeting in the corridor. At this meeting, my lecture changed.

"Ask no one to do for you. There is no God who does for us. Neither is there a Buddha who does for us. No one can play the self-authority. Every individual person must be self-responsible. We must deeply recognize the truth of self-authority; I must admit that. Worshipping, going to temple or making a pilgrimage goes against the truth of self-responsibility. The authority of life is truly self-responsibility. Deny the thought that there will be someone who can save us or who can do for use. If that were so, why would our ancestors need to leave their precious methods of self-cultivation for us? They just led us to what they had discovered. All sages and developed ones are self-responsible for their own development and extend their self-development to other people. Self-awareness is a deep sense of responsibility. If self-awareness causes you to become selfish or assuming, then your self-awareness is incomplete. Complete awareness makes you become fully aware of self-responsibility. Therefore, deny all wishful thinking, but be self-responsible."

At this time, I discovered my mother in the corridor. She smiled, awaiting the conclusion of my lecture. I finished, "Each life is self-responsible on all high levels, especially for individual spiritual development. We must continue self-improvement and pursue the ancient secret way of high achievement that has been left for us. Through self-cultivation, one can reach the true authority of the non-authority, the Tao. Otherwise, all speeches are just empty words. Therefore, my endeavors must be in this direction. It may be after years of cultivating that I can serve people who are self-responsible."

My mother then took me in to the dinner she had made and quietly watched me eat a hearty meal.

Chapter 35

The Development of Life

Without proof of spiritual reality through direct contact with the existence of the vast spiritual realm, a true audience from high divine beings, and the experiencing of divine immortality before exuviating the fleshly life, one's striving toward spiritual development is only partially fulfilled. The gift of expressible, sudden enlightenment does not bring about this fulfillment. Nor will intensive effort in the realm of personal growth techniques or religious practices necessarily lead one closer to the true immortal, divine world. You may, in fact, some day find that you have merely been enacting the ideas or principles of another rather than traveling the integral path to true fulfillment.

The blossoming mind will wither if it does not reunite with its true nature. You may feel that you have arrived at the root of universal life, but without the confirmation of the real experiences mentioned above, your spiritual development is similar to riding an elevator in a tall building. Though the elevator works, the doors open to nowhere.

True achievement comes from obtaining the true method. Taoist practical cultivation, therefore, uses the expressible development that one has attained to serve the public and thereby integrate individual attainment as part of the whole. The main goal of methodical Taoist cultivation is the attainment of immortal life.

Do you believe there are immortals in the universe? By believing, how does one know that he is not being self-deceived? Surely, there must be a way. Yes, there are ways to be taught in the Taoist tradition. One way is the Taoist Sacred Way of Summoning and Connecting with Divine Beings. This method does not belong to the categories of hypnosis, witchcraft, modern parapsychology, psychic powers or religious theology. After learning this method and practicing the cultivation, one can directly and truthfully connect with, and thus summon pure spirits.

After sure-footed proof, one can know that the vast spiritual realm, in general, is divided into the categories of yin and yang. The yin category includes "general beings" of an ordinary life who may or may not have followed a particular religion. The yang category includes "true beings" of the universal eternal life who have attained total freedom and happiness. To receive such a universal citizenship, one must know all the methods of the tradition of the integral immortal beings. The traditional tuition is 1,000 ounces of pure gold. If you think that this price is too high, then the traditional measure of two hundred "catties" of pure gold will do. (One "catty" is about as heavy as an adult cat and is a traditional Chinese pound with 16 ounces.) But, the teaching can also be a reward to a virtuous individual.

Another method is the Secret Carriage to the Immortal Realm. This cultivation is one of the highest Taoist secrets. Understanding this practice can enable one to enter the eternal divine realm, both before and after the exuviation of the fleshly body. After receiving and practicing this method, one establishes sure communication with the different levels of divine immortals and starry beings. Thus, one may become a member of the divine immortal world even during one's physical life. One who discovers and obtains this method shall be successfully saved from a "wasteful" life.

Having no subtle beings is not the world's problem; instead, the problem is too few people with accurately developed spiritual sensitivity. Having too few people who can know subtle things is not the world's problem; instead, the problem is having people who lack the knowledge that there are vast, different spiritual realms. Without the correct methods and practices, one is likely to become lost in the profound spiritual world. In the spiritual world, only the quality of chi of a person's cultivation is recognized. Nothing else should be valued, except the cultivation of chi. Specifically, nothing else in life should be valued but the cultivation of high qualities of chi. Different chi produces differences in people. The quality of chi that one will reach within a lifetime can be anticipated by the path one follows.

There are many valuable, secret methods of Taoist cultivation. All the effective methods have been introduced by Pao Po Tzu, an ancient Taoist with a great heart, in a book entitled *The Pao Po Tzu*. Unfortunately, it has not yet been correctly translated into English. (The book was written during the Chin Dynasty, 265-416 A.D.) Pao Po Tzu's book contains a good introduction to over two thousand ancient, secret methods. I give his biography in *The Life and Teaching of Two Immortals: Kou Hong*. It may draw a sketch of his work.

The truth of all sacred, secret methods of the Taoist tradition can be verified by one who correctly understands them. However, one must have the correct development to receive these special instructions. Not surprisingly, most of these instructions are strongly guarded and prohibited in order to prevent people from immaturely or prematurely practicing them. As a result, the highest treasures of wisdom and technique are limited in their exposure to the world. Because ordinary opportunities to learn these methods do not exist, a long, long time is required to educate a good Taoist toward true development and attainment. Only when a person is truly ready to receive the high spiritual methods will they be passed on. Only then will a student be benefitted rather than endangered. This prohibition also extends to the master, who would also suffer if instructions were given prematurely by him or her to someone else.

A safe and broad way to approach becoming ready to learn the advanced methods is available in my work entitled *The Heavenly Way*, which has been supplemented and reprinted as *The Key to Good Fortune: Refining Your Spirit*. This book contains three treatises. The first, "Straighten Your Way," was Pao Po Tzu's recommendation from his Master and the Masters before his Master. The second article is the traditional elucidation of Chapter 71 of the *Tao Teh Ching*. It says:

> "To know what one knows
> is to be highly enlightened.
> To not know what one should know is sick.
> Only the one sick of suffering
> can be saved from the sickness.
> The highly enlightened one is never sick;
> he is aware of sickness and, therefore, avoids it."

The third article, an exemplification from a deity with human experience, contains the invaluable essence of safe practice. The standard and evaluation for what one must accomplish in preparation for becoming a virtuous person is accurately expressed in these three treatises. Actually, they serve as the Direct Way. And, at that, even one with the extraordinary luck of obtaining the methods as revealed in the above-mentioned treatises still needs virtuous achievement as a foundation of personal energy to attain eternal life.

Wisdom and Safety

The background of the fifth line of the 36th hexagram, Ming Yi, ䷣ is a series of events which took place during the reign of the Emperor Jou (reign 1154-1122 B.C.), the last emperor of the Shang Dynasty (1766-1122 B.C.). It is also a story of how Korea began its history as a nation.

As a youth, Jou was receptive to the teachings of the wise counselors of his father's court. However, he eventually became overly confident of his own abilities and grew tired of the advice of his teachers and counselors. Thinking he was wise enough to rule alone and make his own decisions, he rejected the teachings of the virtuous way. The following is the legendary story of his excesses and corruption.

During one of the national festivals, Emperor Jou, along with the ministers of his court, went on a pilgrimage to the temple of a Heavenly goddess. The statue of the goddess was so beautiful that the Emperor became entranced. He believed that, since he was Emperor, the goddess would come to him and be his woman. This blasphemous, licentious wish actually manifested in the form of a real woman, Tan Chi, who later became Emperor Jou's favorite. After taking Tan Chi into his confidence, he would not accept advice from anyone else. With this, the downfall and destruction of his empire began.

Separated from the correct path of life, Emperor Jou began to follow an extravagant lifestyle. Consideration for his country and everything else was lost in his constant desire to please his mistress. The demands placed on his people were extreme. Ponds were built in his court and filled with wine. His people were ordered to give him their best meat, which was hung on the trees of his garden for Tan Chi and her horde of attendants to enjoy. Beautiful girls were forced to pose nude as a human screen where he sat. He even built a great tower in hopes that the stars could be picked for her pleasure. He had his first wife put to death, and eventually his empire became corrupt. He was also cruel to the ministers who had faithfully served him and his father.

One day, Tan Chi feigned illness. Although Emperor Jou ordered the doctors to help her, she did not respond to their treatment. Tan Chi told the Emperor that in order for her to become healthy again she must drink blood from the loyal heart of his key minister, who also happened to be his uncle. Not being able to refuse her, Emperor Jou ordered his loyal minister, Pi Kan, to allow his heart to be cut out as a demonstration of his allegiance to the Emperor. This order was given on an occasion when Pi Kan had advised the Emperor to desert Tan Chi and tend to affairs of state. Pi Kan faithfully accepted the Emperor's order, and Emperor Jou subsequently did the same thing to many other loyal ministers who advised him in a similar manner after being instructed by Tan Chi to kill them. The remaining wise ministers, whose lives had thus far been spared, faced a serious moral dilemma. Being deceitful in order to please the Emperor was against their conscience and way of life. However, if they offered honest advice, they would surely be killed.

The old premier, Wen, after returning home from an assigned expedition, felt that his duty was to correctly advise the Emperor. Wen informed him that he should not devote himself to Tan Chi, but instead should offer his devotion to his country. Because of Wen's outstanding military achievements, the Emperor hesitated to kill him, and his life was temporarily spared. When Tan Chi discovered what Wen had said and how the Emperor let him off, she devised a plan that would create doubt in Emperor Jou's mind about the loyalty of his premier. Her plan was to heat the inside of a hollow brass pillar and ask the premier to prove his loyalty by embracing it. The Emperor declared that, if Wen were genuinely faithful, he would not die. The premier could not refuse the test and embraced the red-hot pillar. However, just before dying, he cried out to the young emperor, "I will see that your kingdom is eliminated from the Earth! I choose this day for my death, while the Earth is still clean and not yet totally spoiled by you!"

Emperor Jou had another uncle, Chi Tzu, who was an *I Ching* practitioner. Chi Tzu was inspired by this hexagram. King Wen later followed his example in order to stay safe from the jealousy of Emperor Jou by acting ignorant. Chi Tzu realized that he could not overcome the power of Jou's darkness by revealing his truthful light. Therefore, he decided not to say anything to Jou and do something that would save his life. He feigned madness by running around naked, dancing in the streets, gambling, losing money he did not own and selling himself to his creditors. He became like a degraded slave and acted as though he enjoyed it. In this way, he was able to stay alive. This is why Lao Tzu says, "High wisdom looks like stupidity." But I would say that high wisdom includes stupidity. That is my personal excuse.

When Tan Chi asked the Emperor if any of his loyal ministers were still alive, the Emperor replied that there were none except Chi Tzu, who was completely useless. After a time, however, Chi Tzu went to the region of Korea, where he was established as a feudal prince by the new dynasty. Seeing the national flag of South Korea today, it is clear how much the *I Ching* influenced Chi Tzu and his descendants. There is a red and blue Tai Chi symbol and the eight hexagrams of the Ba Gua on the flag.

Emperor Jou's psychological problem was an obsession to prove his abilities by going beyond his father's influence. But he abused his power and became too strong. His life was a great example of excess and imbalance, which manifested in an extremely negative manner. He ultimately lost his empire and took his own life by burning himself to death.

The fifth line of the 36th hexagram tells a sage's conduct when he faced a dangerous and dark situation. The above story of Jou tells the background that the sage faced. In normal situations, wisdom is respected. In the time of darkness, wisdom would invite danger to life. Chi Tzu was the only person whose conduct was appropriate in this situation of darkness.

The first version of the *I Ching* had no written text, only the symbols of the hexagrams. Ken Wen, a feudal prince during the reign of Emperor Jou, began to write a text to accompany it. Emperor Jou was intimidated by the reputed abilities of King Wen and was determined to find out if he truly had the power of foreknowledge. King Wen was then summoned and confined to the capital. As a secret test, Emperor Jou had the King's son killed and then served the boy's flesh in a soup. King Wen knew that to refuse the soup would prove he had foreknowledge of his son's death, so he drank it, passed the test to the Emperor's satisfaction and was released.

King Wen became the "seed of fire" for the upcoming revolution that would begin a new dynasty.

The following story is yet another illustration of dealing with the time of darkness. At the end of the Chou Dynasty (1122-256 B.C.), there lived a famous Master, "Son of the Spiritual Valley," who had two students. The elder student was advanced in his studies, while the younger student, who was quite handsome, was rather negligent in his. The young, handsome student left his Master and traveled west to the State of We, where he became a general and married King Wei's daughter. The king placed the young man in charge of the entire army that was going to attack the neighboring state of Chi.

Some time later, the King heard that the elder student was superior in wisdom and invited him to the court as an advisor. The wise Master, knowing that this situation would be dangerous, warned his elder student. However, the student thought, "I came to learn from you, Master, but now I have an opportunity to use what I have learned in governing the affairs of state. Please allow me to take this honorable position." Although the Master advised his student that this was an inappropriate time for such an assignment, he realized that the student was intent on leaving. Before he departed, the Master said, "I have a secret letter for you. If you encounter extreme difficulty, open it and follow the directions inside. You will then be safe. But only in the most dangerous situation should the envelope be opened!"

The elder student then became King Wei's respected guest and was treated with much favor. It soon became apparent that he had more depth than the younger student, the King's son-in-law. The younger student, realizing how the king felt, knew that if something were not done soon, he would lose his position as general. Therefore, he told the king that the elder student's hometown was in the State of Chi and that he should not be told of the plan to attack it because he might be a spy. The king listened to this logic, agreed with the younger student, and put the elder student in prison in order to observe him. It was clear to the elder student how dangerous his situation had become and that his teacher's warnings were coming true. Remembering the letter given to him by his teacher, he quickly opened it. On the page was written only one word, "Mad." He then knew that to survive, he must appear to be insane.

For a while the king's men observed the elder student intensely, but as his madness continued the king eventually lost interest. The young student, realizing that his purpose was accomplished, now felt safe. However, because the king was negligent in guarding the older student, he was able to escape. His foot had been cut off under King Wei's order, and he was filthy from having slept in the dirt. Nevertheless, he was rescued and carried by wagon to Chi where he became a close advisor to their king. He successfully protected that state and carried it to victory by his brilliant military strategy. Unavoidably, the great commander of Wei (the younger, handsome student) was defeated, losing both his army and his life. The older, wiser student, whose name was Sun Tse, whose book on military strategy, the popular *Art of War*, became one of the most influential works in history. The successful Japanese businessmen respect it as a holy book for running their businesses. The Japanese inherited their cultural heritage from China; they share the same cultural background.

Spiritual Opportunity is Equal to All

Cultivate the Tao as your own spiritual integrity,
and you need not worry about producing
the proper fruit.
Once one's root is well taken care of,
good fruit is the natural result.
Life is all equal to anyone.
A sage has neither more nor less spiritual integrity
when he was born
than a mediocre man
when he was born.
No different are the rich and poor,
the noble and the common.
The difference between them lies
in how they make use of their will or intention.

If you can adhere to the sacred method,
cultivating yourself precisely,
keeping clear as to your every motive and idea,
then all good, positive qualities
become firm and all traps can be avoided.
This is called correct use of the will.
You then become one with Tao,
unchanged even in death
as you realize the eternal firmness of existence.
You will grow a spiritual body.
This undecayed, everlasting spiritual body
is the highest true soul
which connects to the source of the universe.

Because the great harmony of non-action -
different from no-action -
has such wondrous effects,
the spiritual firmness of Tao is reached
by the sincerity of daily life.
Impartiality is the key.

With it you remove all cause for worry
over excessive conduct.
This is the correct and sacred way of a shien.
Cling to it firmly, strictly and finally.
The sprouting seed of a whole being
makes steady growth.

Chapter 37

Virtue in Family Life

Female and male in harmony
*   are the strong foundation of a happy marriage.*
When choosing a mate,
*   outer beauty is not necessary,*
*   but virtuous behavior is.*

If one's heart is good,
*   noble children will be born.*
Hand down the right instructions to them
*   and be strict, softened by gentleness.*
Do not possess your offspring,
*   but guide them to form their character*
*   so that they can stand alone*
*   when their time comes.*
They will carry forth your virtuous behavior
*   as their heritage,*
*   and in turn will guide the next generation*
*   on the right path.*
Be aware that your example
*   carries through many generations to come.*
When instructing your children,
*   example is better than precept.*
It is better to keep their lives as simple as possible.
Even if you are prosperous,
*   keep them always a little hungry and a little cold.*
It is a challenge in this affluent society
*   to restrain oneself*
*   and live as if there were no abundance.*
Spoiled children become weak adults.
Self-indulgence is the greatest misery of our times.

Limit your activities and those of your children.
Too many activities scatter their developing minds.
Make the home inviting
*   with quiet activities and togetherness.*

Television is the biggest threat to a developing mind
and brings disorder to the family.
Cut your own desire,
    and the desire of your children will lessen.
Teach them to be content with little.

Let them be aware of caring for others,
    as well as for themselves and the environment.
Your children, when young,
    need to feel secure and loved.
Regularity and steadfastness on your part
    gives them security.
Strictness, softened by gentleness and forgiveness,
    makes them feel loved.
With these two virtues,
    the foundation for the harmonious development
    of their being is built.

Dare to stand back and watch
    their unfolding growth process,
    with reserve and respect for their own natures,
    interfering only at the right time.
Give them time and space to develop
    in accordance with their own divine plan.
In the early years it is easy to observe
    their divine natures,
    but soon the whole picture of their inheritance
    and self-created life patterns accumulated
    through many lifetimes will emerge.
We must stand by to exercise and encourage
    the positive side of their characters
    and encourage them to recognize and change
    their negative tendencies.

Use firmness and discipline,
    always softened by gentleness.
Form a Tai Chi in everything you do.
Find the balance in interacting with your children.
Bring yin and yang into harmony in your own person.

To have a harmonious family,
  each member must be aware of his or her place.
If roles are reversed between male and female,
  disharmony is the inevitable result.
Great confusion starts in families
  when people use forceful means
  to insure their identities.
The evolution of the human race as a whole
  requires adjustment from both partners
  in a mature and gentle way.
Positively approached,
  we must grow in a flexible yin-yang relationship,
  giving both partners room for their personal growth,
  each fulfilling their role within their natures.

The wife's place is predominantly in the home,
  her nature being to shelter and nurture.
The husband's place is predominantly
  outside of the home,
  his nature being to provide and support.
The oldest child should teach the youngest;
  the youngest should follow the oldest.
In this way, harmony can be established.
Respect for the other person, young or old,
  should be the key word within
  and without your family.
Respect nurtures kindness.
With kindness you can win the hearts of the people.
Maintain economy without being stingy.
When you are careful and practical in monetary affairs,
  you have much to give away.
Never hoard money for selfish purposes.

In the family, cultivate the outer aspects of
  conscientiousness, respect and gentleness.
The practical aspects of the home are
  tolerance, flexibility and patience.
These virtues will make your home
  a shelter for all those who may enter.
People will move about contented with their own beings.

Natural affection will brighten their days.
Cultivate respect,
  follow the laws of nature,
  and abide in the principles of Tao.
Then your life will be useful, calm and fulfilling,
  and life's abundance will display itself within you.
When that happens, it will be found
  within the family,
  within your neighborhood,
  within your community,
  within the state,
  within the country,
  and ultimately within the whole world.
Such is the way.
Such is the law of subtle energy response.

Chapter 38

The Sacred Seed of a Whole Being

Ordinary worldly religions and teachings
  attract ordinary minds.
Their tenets, like haphazard vines,
  sprawl every which way.
Illusory and idealistic,
  they attempt to explain reality,
  but fall short,
  unable to penetrate
  their own spiritual blind spot.
They attract weak spirits
  who must cling to something
  stronger than themselves,
  who must encourage consoling illusions
  to cheat themselves.

Follow this crude way of trusting and believing,
  without self-development,
  and what you will experience is but a void.
After you experience the truth,
  you will know why shien cultivation
  emphasizes self-realization and transformation.
Therein lies the answer
  to the puzzle of oral and written obstacles.

First, strengthen yourself,
  then you can influence your environment.
All parts of your body and spirit
  will become like hands and eyes.
Develop your mental ability
  until it is round,
  full and smooth as a pearl.
Then reap the reward.
Fearing danger no more,
  you will easily shake free of its bondage.

The subtle heavenly law
    will appear within you and through you
    because you have succeeded
    in the spirit of gentleness.
Truly, even while living in the world,
    you will come to surpass and transcend
    its mundane problems and difficulties.

Divine awareness always appears,
    helping you as you go,
    while leaving your spiritual ego
    in union with all beings.
Heaven, Earth and I are a union of one,
    for we are of the same origin.
Realize this
    and become the strong seed
    of a whole being.

Chapter 39

Work to Refine Your Precious Wisdom

To cultivate the Tao, spiritual integrity,
* you must first exalt purity.*
Clean the mind of all stains.
Frequently review your judgments.
Hold firm to the pure motives
* which inspired your cultivation.*
Bar the entrance of evil disturbances.
Do not allow the mind to change.
Even on the roughest roads,
* keep it steadfast as it travels*
* toward its destination.*
Let it not float, move or trap itself.

It is uncleanliness of body and mind
* that causes the disorders of passion and virtue.*
Disorder makes peace impossible.
Evil powers are divisible by four:
* external, internal,*
* apparent and hidden.*
The most difficult are the hidden,
* because your knowledge of their coming*
* is prevented.*
You must recognize them
* in their subtle beginnings.*
Work to refine your precious wisdom,
* and you will not need to retreat*
* from the world to avoid its temptations.*
Your all-important balance
* is damaged by too much inharmonious*
* mental activity.*
If mental disorder arises,
* you are the evil powers' slave.*
Of the few principles in cultivating Tao,
* the key one is keeping your real mind pure,*
* undivided, unscattered.*

Self-discipline alone
   will correctly develop your divine nature.
The subtle body,
   which will manifest itself,
   is the basis of your immortality.
It is possible to become a thief
   of your own balance.
Have caution on the road you travel
   to become a whole being.

Chapter 40

Self-Composure can Change Misfortune
Into Good Fortune

To become one with Tao,
*   or to become a shien, an immortal being,*
*   newly achieved and born in heaven,*
*   there is one, only one requirement:*
*   keep a consistently calm mind.*
Keep it peaceful, transparent and
*   still as the water of a clear, quiet lake,*
*   and you will enjoy the subtlety of great bliss.*
When dealing with
*   minor problems or major disasters,*
*   stay calm and still as a holy mountain.*
When dealing with the pleasurable,
*   maintain strict discipline.*
In this way,
*   when the unpleasant presents itself,*
*   your mind will not be disturbed.*

Those who would embellish rites and rituals,
*   succeed only in trying to impress others.*
There is no power to be gained.
Nor is self-cultivation a tool
*   for exacting respect from your community.*
It must show its effectiveness
*   on all occasions,*
*   especially in times of great difficulty.*
Every day, in each ordinary situation,
*   you can realize the benefit of self-cultivation.*
No special time is reserved for this.
The calm power derived from your daily practice
*   can transform what seems to be a disaster*
*   into a blessing.*
Quietude can change misfortune into good fortune.
Understand the elusive quality of your body and mind.

It is easy to keep the mind calm and the emotions
  peaceful in ordinary situations,
  but how difficult it is when problems come!
Learn this and you will be qualified
  to sit in the seat of the Lotus,
  to look deep within yourself.

Be as person of iron -
  your mind firm, unshakable -
  and you will become the favorite child
  of the family of whole beings.

Chapter 41

Absolute Freedom

Living in the world, we are sometimes benefitted through increase. At other times, we are benefitted by decrease. As Chapter 48 of the *Tao Teh Ching* says:

"In learning, the increase of knowledge
and skill should be seen daily.
In cultivation, the decrease of coarseness
in character and impurity in mind
should also be seen daily
in order to reach the true essence."

Spiritual truth is derived from the unfolding of a natural mind. Such an experience can be described as the complete "opening" of the mind, like a fully-blossoming flower - totally liberating the mind, untying the entanglements of the mind, unveiling the truth or revelation of the ultimate truth. All of these terms carry the same connotation but differ vastly with personal experience. Such practices and pursuits of spiritual achievement are high above common religious worship.

Among all the great books ever written about the nature of truth, Chuang Tzu's is the highest. His teachings, however, are difficult to translate. Unfortunately, there was no correct translation available to English speaking people before. This fact is not due to English sinologists being unskilled, but it is like using an oil painting technique to copy a Chinese brush-painted masterpiece. The work of art can be well-copied and may look the same; however, to the eye which has seen the original, a distinction can be made between its authenticity and the copied work. A translation cannot convey the original Taoist unobstructed spirit. Also, the original book itself is easily misunderstood. Thus, not only could one incorrectly interpret its effect, but one's thinking might be contorted as well.

Among the hundreds of thousands of readers of that great book, perhaps only one will be able to restore his original nature. Why? Because merely reading a book and getting a vague impression of its meaning without the direct training and guidance of a truly achieved one is not enough. It is difficult to reach the level of an achieved master. Furthermore, it is not a matter of understanding, but a way of living. One can follow nothing until one has experienced the real model. People in their general lives and religious practices have specific ways of expressing what they do, such as a cook, a carpenter, a farmer, a teacher or a minister. However, a Taoist master has no trace of anything discernible. From him you see nothing.

Has anyone ever seen a real dragon? A real dragon does not show itself. How can people with undeveloped eyes see the really achieved one? They only see his human shape. Seeing him is less interesting than seeing an attractive move star! Moreover, there is no benefit from just seeing a really achieved one. Spiritual benefit is not based on one's understanding - it is based on direct reunion with the subtle truth. A person who says he knows that someone is a Taoist master does not know the master at all. This person covers himself with shallowness. This is like the many attempts to make "Chuang Tzu" a subject to be studied. Learning Tao is not like studying someone. Tao is not to be understood. Tao is just what is.

Once I wrote some Chinese calligraphy in strong, black ink on a piece of paper and put it on the wall of my study. It read:

> *"I sit with vulgar people.*
> *I stand with vulgar people.*
> *But where I live*
> *is not where vulgar people can reach!"*

I truly believed that I had achieved this. My elder sister happened to see the writing, and on one occasion, she and my younger brother found an opportunity to quiz me about it during dinner one summer evening. (We were all teenagers at this time.) Hoping to shake me from my diamond throne of spiritual achievement, she began this way:

"You use big characters to tell the world that you sit
with vulgar people and that you stand with vulgar people,
but is it not we who sit and stand with you? Since the
writing refers to 'us' as vulgar people, then what are you?"

My younger brother continued, "Where you live is not
where vulgar people can reach! But to us, living under the
same roof means that you are the same as us!"

This was one of the "wars" in which I was under attack
because of my own foolish "achievement." Thus I had
invited this invasion.

Our eldest sister never failed to act as an arbitrator, as
she did on this occasion. She said, "Be quiet. He means
that his spirit no longer follows this same vulgar track."

"We doubt that he is achieved in such a way that distin-
guishes him from us!" my second sister and young brother
sang in unison.

"You only reveal your own vulgarity by insisting on interfering with his personal spiritual endeavor!" my eldest
sister said.

Although my eldest sister thankfully saved me from
embarrassment, I still did not fully realize my mistake.
When the defeated "knight" retreated to the kitchen, my
mother was already washing the dishes. As she worked, she
repeatedly murmured, "Everything is Tao. Everything is not
Tao." I thought she might be trying to teach me to recognize
that kitchen work is also the performance of Tao, as she
often did. However, in front of my mother, I acted like a
little child again. I started to touch everything in our old-
fashioned Chinese kitchen. Every time I touched something
I would say, "This is Tao, that is Tao," and continued to do
so until there was nothing more that I could put my finger
on. After I stopped my frivolous actions, my mother said,
"What you can touch is the Tao with form. Show me the
unformed Tao."

For a moment I was dumfounded. Then, pointing at the
empty space I said, "This is Tao, that is Tao."

My mother simply said, "No, this is East and that is
South."

Then I moved my finger in all different directions and
said, "This is Tao. That is Tao." But everywhere I pointed,

my mother proclaimed the direction and the space, such as left and right, front and rear, upper and lower, and so forth. There was no place my finger pointed without direction or name. I hastily pointed at myself and then at her. I continued to be given a name, a form, a describable being or a definable meaning. Finally, I gave up. There was no hope of expressing the unformed Tao. She gave me time to collect myself, but by now, I had tried everything in vain.

Then my mother said with a slow and clear voice, "Since your 'Tao' is with form, you bind yourself with your own vulgar triviality. How can you enjoy the absolute freedom of being with Tao? Tao is neither with form, nor is it formless. This is why I repeated to you, 'Everything is Tao, everything is not Tao.'"

At that moment I received a new light which pierced the darkness of my self imposed cocoon. My mother led me to discover the imperfection of spiritual achievement.

During the following months I completely reworked myself without mercy. During that Winter, around the time of the Chinese New Year, it began to snow. We stopped most outdoor activities and gathered in the kitchen, my mother's "empire."

My mother asked me to express my yearly achievement by writing a poem with snow as the topic. I wrote:

> *There is no trace of snow when it is fine.*
> *There is no trace of being fine when it snows.*
> *Before the birth of Heaven and Earth,*
>   *neither trace could be found.*

I read the poem to my mother. She then asked me to present it to my father. My father read it with a smile. After I repeatedly insisted on having his comment, he finally said, "I am happy to see that you can connect all changing events to the unchangeable, true nature of the universe, but your poem lacks the vividness of life. Such beliefs could lead to the narrow practice of a religion. Tao is life. If Tao is what you choose, then come back to the real life!"

In this moment, and with the help of my father's seldom-used mystical sword, the thick layer of my mental obstruction was peeled away. Thus, I immediately received true freedom from spiritual bondage. My gain was not from my father's words. My "half-achievement" was to stick with the fine day mind and refuse the troubled weather mind. This is not real achievement. It was a lofty and stagnant thought of attachment to peace.

In later years, due to the drastic changes in the world I was in another place, far away from our old home. Undaunted, I shouldered the responsibility of passing the truth as a healing, awakening means for individuals to cultivate an integral life. In this endeavor I met tremendous difficulties from all directions, but with the innermost light of my true nature, I overcame all obstacles (which actually stirred my growth). On one occasion, I had a chance to write to my elderly father to assure him that in all aspects of life, I was all right. I wrote him in the wintertime, after the snow had fallen in the high mountains. I missed my family very much and was especially worried about my parents who, at that time, were living under tremendous pressures. Finally I got an answer from my father. In his letter he wrote:

> *"When it is fine, I am trouble-free.*
> *When it is snowing, I am also trouble-free.*
> *No matter how the world changes,*
> *I always remain trouble-free."*

He expressed his unobstructed spirit in this poem during a time of the adversity of the Chinese nation.

Generally, when people have a comfortable life, their natures are buried under material enjoyment. When they live under adversity, their natures are bent and damaged. Those of real achievement can not only enjoy comforts, but can also withstand adversity. Clouds do not really hinder the sky, and neither does the sky hinder the clouds. The real usefulness of spiritual achievement is similar to drinking water - only the one who drinks shall know the true flavor.

Chapter 42

Attaining a Practical Mind

Everyone looks for benefits and favors for one's life, but does one really know what is beneficial and favorable? The true essence of life is chi. It is chi that builds life. One who would truly develop the vision to know this truth, should be willing to engage in the cultivation of chi.

What is chi? Chi is the mother of all things and all beings. It is the subtle essence of the universe. This statement could never satisfy an ordinary intellectual mind, but the use of the mind represents only one way in which chi moves. Recognition of the deep truth depends on long years of self-reflection and cultivation. Through actual cultivation, one can discover the subtle existence of chi.

In order to seriously begin the cultivation of chi, a peaceful mind is necessary. This should be practiced not with a passive purpose, but with a positive and creative purpose. In human life, a peaceful mind can nurture personal vitality. Here is where all personal enterprises of spiritual and worldly achievement start.

Sometimes knowing how much progress one is making is not easy, but the following discussion might help you obtain your preliminary goal.

Conceptual recognition of the contradictory nature of worldly things comes from mental objectivity, but this does not help eliminate the conflicts that are experienced in real life. Thus, conceptual development may only be helpful as a first step. The way taught by ancient Taoists for attaining a peaceful, undisturbed and unattached mind is the withdrawal of one's mental being from the outer layer of worldly tensions to the unified core of universal life.

A peaceful, undisturbed and unexcitable mind can be achieved by nurturing chi. A dialogue between Mencius and one of his students explains this important practice. (Mencius, a popular teacher in China, who lived from 372 B.C. to 289 B.C., was a student of Confucius during Confucius' later years.)

"Master, if you were put in the position of the premier of the State of Chi so that you could fulfill all good principles as you had always wished, you would be the equal of a king dealing with major affairs of state. Would this opportunity excite you?" inquired the student.

"No," said Mencius. "When I was forty, I had already achieved an undisturbed mind."

"Then," said the student, "you must have surpassed even the ancient brave man, Men Pei, who did not fear anything on land or in water. Richness, nobility or even fear for his own life did not disturb his unexcitable mind."

Mencius replied, "It should not be so difficult. Kao Tzu, your fellow student, achieved a passionless, undisturbed mind even earlier than I."

"Master, is there any sure way of reaching a passive, undisturbed mind?" queried the student.

Mencius said, "There are several ways. Pei Kung Yu's method was to control the skin and not react to heat, cold or pain. His eyelids did not blink with any agitation, and he did not turn his face or close his eyes to anything fearful. But if one single hair on his body was damaged by anyone, he would become as insulted as if he were publicly beaten. It did not matter whether that person was in ordinary clothes or a king of ten thousand chariots, his revenge was taken in defensive action. If bad words were spoken to him, then the same would be returned by him. This was his way of keeping the vigor of his mind.

"The method of Men Shih Shr was to face defeat as one would face victory. He estimated the enemy before marching and measured the chance of triumph before engaging in war. He said, 'I do not let my mind think I am the winner, but neither do I let fear disturb me.'

"These are but two ways among many to achieve an undisturbed mind. The first way, that of Pei Kung Yu, suggests facing bad situations fearlessly. In other words, exerting the vigor of the mind instead of depressing it. The second way, that of Men Shih Shr, stresses the centering of one's mind before putting it to good use. I cannot say which is the stronger way, although I do think that Men Shih Shr's way may be more practical.

"I remember Tsen Tzu taught one of his students the following, 'You wish to be powerful? I heard my master, Confucius, say that, when the most powerful one inquires into a matter with his mind and finds out what is not right, even if he faces a simple, ordinary person, he still feels fear. If he inquires into a matter with his mind and finds out what is right, even if there are thousands and thousands of people who say it is wrong, he still faces it."

Mencius continued, "From viewing this, I think Tsen Tzu's way is the most important."

The student asked, "Master, may I venture to ask your way of cultivation and how it differs from Kao Tzu's way? You mentioned that he achieved his undisturbed mind earlier than you, but he has followed you for some time."

Mencius responded, "Kao Tzu's principle for reaching an unperturbed mind is this: 'Do not think about the unjust words people speak to you and do not resort to emotions when people disagree with you.' The main guidance of his way is 'do not.' But from my understanding, the rational mind is the center. The emotional force is connected to the whole body. When the rational mind reacts to a situation, the emotional force follows. Therefore, keep the rational mind peaceful and do not violently stir passion."

"Master, you have pointed out that when the rational mind reacts to a situation, emotional force follows. It seems that the whole matter is the mind. But you also say to keep the rational mind in peace and to not violently stir the passion," said the student.

Mencius replied, "When the mind is in control, it 'moves' the emotions, but when the emotions are in control, they 'move' the mind. For instance, when one who has been walking falls down and becomes angry, it is emotion that moves the mind."

"Master, may I venture to ask the advantage of your way?" queried the student.

Mencius responded, "I think, first of all, that I understand people's words and the meaning behind all that is said. I especially cultivate the boundless inner power of personality in order to maintain the unperturbed mind."

"Master, may I venture to ask, what is the meaning of the boundless inner power of personality?" asked the student.

"This is difficult to express; however, this power is the greatest and the mightiest. It can only be successfully nurtured in a peaceful and harmless mind by using righteousness and by following the Way. Thus, it can extend to any sphere of the universe. Otherwise, it evaporates. Why? Because the power is obtained by accumulating righteousness and the correct way of life. It cannot be obtained by occasional righteousness. When one's behavior does not agree with one's mind, then this power becomes deflated.

"Therefore, I think Kao Tzu has not known that the power is within us. Cultivating this power must be done with gentle care. There is no room for negligence, nor is there anything extra to do in order to help it grow.

"Do not do as the person who lived in the State of Sung. He thought his young crops did not grown fast enough, so he went to the fields to pull them up a bit higher. Quickly finishing his work, he returned to his family. He told them, 'I am so tired now. I helped all the crops grow today.' His father went to the fields to see them, but they had all wilted."

From this dialogue we can understand that Mencius' undisturbed mind is not a negative practice but a power that is nurtured within. This boundless power can be cultivated by a pacified mind. Mencius was benefitted by his own cultivation and he lived more than ninety years, smoothly, wisely, healthily and successfully.

From Mencius one can have a complete understanding of cultivating Tao. One does not need to do anything extra, but one should keep away from all negative things.

Chapter 43

The True Mind

The main guidance for becoming an integral being is: "If even one small portion of yin energy (the dualistic function of the mind) remains, then one will not become a shien. If even one small portion of yang energy (the integralness of life) is not complete, one will not become a shien."

In the science of self-cultivation, chi belongs to the yang category and mind belongs to the yin category. All thoughts are a digression from one's essence, and essence is what enables one to maintain wholeness.

In the hexagram Kui,☰, Resolute Change, the yang energy can be completed only when the remaining yin line on the top is eliminated. In self-cultivation, only when the untruthful mind is regulated can the wholeness of spiritual life be attained. Let the following discussion probe our minds.

To wonder if there is a God or no God is a typical question of the dualistic mind which can only respond with "yes" or "no." If you look deeply enough, you will find that the true nature of the mind is not dualistic, nor is the true nature of the universe. The self-nature of the universe can be called God.

Look at the mind. It is hardly substantial. It reveals itself only through its function and work. The most insubstantial deep mind is called the true mind. Tracing this, one is able to enter the formless realm of the life of the universe which never ceases. With it, the universe operates in an organic way and is identified as subtle law.

If a person only recognizes his mind as being important, then what is the importance of the brain? If a person only recognizes the universal mind as being important to life, then what is the importance of matter? If you can give up the juggling of both ideas, you may find Tao. Mind and matter permeate each other and interact well. Looking from the unmanifest truth to manifested matter, one will see things having forms which are limited in truth and short in development. To look from the unmanifest to the manifest sphere, one will not be bewildered by the diversity of forms which derive their essence from the oneness of the subtle origin. The only way to remain integral is to maintain a balance between the unmanifest and manifest spheres of the universe. Who can really deny the oneness of the integral universe?

The following illustrations may be useful in attempting to explore the true mind.

In China, a famous master led a group of students on a hike in the mountains in the early spring. Eventually they came to an unusual place where, to their surprise, they discovered a beautiful peach tree in blossom. Everybody was enchanted by its brilliant rich pinkness and remained silent as they enjoyed its extraordinary beauty. For some time they were unable to take their eyes away from it.

After a long while, the master posed several questions. First he asked, "Is the universe with or without a mind? If it is without a mind, who brings about the beauty? Must not there be a universal mind behind the ordinariness to present such beauty?

"Secondly, if the universe has a mind, should not this tree blossom in the city so that more people could experience its exquisite creation?

"Thirdly, without you and I to experience this tree, does its beauty still have meaning?"

When I was a young man, I formulated answers to these questions as follows: "The self-nature of the universe gives birth to the peach tree and to all beauty. It is the self-nature of the peach tree to produce flowers, as it is the self-nature of people to respond to the beauty of its flowers." Was I correct?

Once, during a time of confusion, a rebellious army came to attack a region of China. Understandably, the people of this region began to flee. Among those refugees was a group of young scholars who passed by a plum garden. The fruit on the trees was red and fully ripened, the branches drooping heavily under their weight. Eagerly, everyone began picking and eating the fruit. Among this group of students, however, was one young man who did not eat the fruit. His companions were surprised and asked him why he did not pick any plums. This garden now, during the time of confusion, belonged to no lord. The young scholar answered, "Truly, the trees and the whole garden belong to no master now, but within each of us there is a master, whether there is one outside of me or not. No irresponsible behavior should be done by a person of responsibility." My beloved friends, was he correct?

The next story is about a young man who fell in love with his cousin. The cousin refused to marry him because of their close blood relationship. Although it was acceptable in ancient China for a cousin on the mother's side to be married to a cousin on the father's side, the young girl still refused the young man's love, and he became greatly saddened. After some time, the young man became rich. In his innermost heart, however, he felt empty and began to desert his current wife and three children. He drank, took drugs and kept a mistress who looked like his cousin. He spent a great deal of money on this girl because of her resemblance to the cousin he had truly loved.

The young man knew that he was squandering his life and money and believed it was solely because of his disappointment in love. Do you believe his reason was real? Then why, when the opportunity to marry his cousin later occurred, did he feel his love no longer existed? Which was real to him, his mind or his love? If his mind was the true love, it could not be altered. True love is supposed to be unalterable. If you decide that love is the true reason, or the reality is a matter of personal growth, it was not the emotion of love which is a passion of needing and wanting and an excuse for personal downfall. Can true love be changed by the passage of time? Is there ever "true love" between men and women? Must true love be expressed by possession? Why does the difficulty of obtaining things always make them more desirable, and why are the most common goods the most valuable in terms of human survival?

The fourth story takes place in a Taoist temple. An old master once declared, "The true mind is not a formed mind. The mind that is formed is just a response to circumstance, thus it is not the unformed, true mind. When sailing on the ocean, one is not aware of smooth water, but when the water becomes rough one quickly notices it. Which part is the true ocean? Which is not?

"The 'false' mind is the conceptual mind that has taken form by reacting to specific situations. What is formed is no longer the 'substance' of the mind - once expressed, it becomes matter. True mind has no shape, no form, no direction and no preference. Ordinary people pay attention only to the reactions and formulations of the conceptual mind and neglect the quietly existing true mind, but one who practices the Integral Way values the original, unformalized mind more than its reactions to specific events. Similarly, people of vulgar religions worship expressed spiritual events while those who practice the Integral Way worship the unexpressed subtleness of integrity."

In the neighborhood of this temple, there happened to be a fox's nest. Foxes are smart animals and they like to imitate humans. One moonlit night the local foxes had a spiritual meeting like that of their Taoist neighbors. The old leader of the foxes, who was sitting in front of the group, began his lecture with "The true mind is not conceptual. The conceptual mind is not the true mind..." and so on, until a dog appeared. At this time, all the foxes rushed away. It is easy to talk like a master, but it is hard to cultivate and maintain an undisturbed, true mind.

The old Taoist master had something more to say, "The wooden fox has a true mind." Do you believe this? If you do, are you an idiot? If you do not, are you a fool? Tell me, what is the truth behind this?

At the age of six, I used to play in the carpentry workshop of a neighbor. He specialized in making round shaped wooden vessels, hence his tools were somewhat different from those of a regular carpenter. One day, I wished to make something of my own and played carelessly with some newly sharpened chisels. Being unskilled at using the tools, I inevitably chiseled my left index finger instead of the wood. It was a deep cut and the finger was almost gone. It bled profusely and was very painful. With my mother watching nervously and my brother and sister surrounding me, I cried bitterly as my father put medicine on the finger and confidently mended it.

My father quietly asked me, "Why do you cry so nervously?"

"It hurts!" I yelped.

"How do you know you are in pain?" he asked.

"I feel it! My mind feels it."

"Then it is pain and not your mind," my father calmly corrected me.

At that time I did not understand what my father said. I was too busy with the pain to ask further questions. Years later my father took my hand, looked at the scar on my left index finger and asked, "Do you feel pain now?"

"Of course not," I replied.

He continued, "Didn't I tell you that it was pain and not the mind? Pain will pass, but not the mind. Ordinary people complain with their mind. An achieved one dissolves the real trouble."

Dear friend, can you give equal attention to the troubled mind and the true mind? Which serves you more? Have you ever known the existence of the true mind as being the quiet, faithful servant of your life being? Yet is it not always neglected by you? You may complain with your mind and exaggerate your troubles, but is it your mind which creates stories to separate you from the truth, or something else which does all of this? Is it the unformed true mind or the false mind which lacks simplicity and clarity that causes you unnecessary confusion? Who should be charged with the responsibility? Can you accurately use your mind? Or does your mind command you? Can you separate the rough waters of the ocean from the peaceful waters, or should one separate the roughness from the peacefulness? In other words, should we create separation between troubles and the mind in spiritual practice? What is the real value of this? Please ask yourself.

Chapter 44

The Untrue Mind

Just as in the hexagram Kou, ☰ where the aggressive yin energy cannot harmonize with the higher yang energy, at a level the mind cannot harmonize with nature and thus the untrue mind is formed. The following story is one of my early experiences in dealing with this problem.

It seems impossible to know the true mind unless you first learn to recognize the untrue mind. Once I asked my father about this. He said that he could help me study the fundamental principles of Chinese medicine, but that the high practice of the traditional healing art could not be put into words. It is a matter of skill achieved through development. In the same manner, the question of true mind is a matter of real achievement and practice, it is not a matter of discussion or gathering information. My father wished for me to discover the answer myself and thus be truly benefitted by my accomplishment.

Because of the frustration of wanting to understand all spiritual truth in one second, I put myself through years of active inquiry, study and experience and so began my spiritual journey. One of those experiences is related in the commentary entitled "Premature Enlightenment." The following experience occurred before my premature enlightenment and was several years before I had received the truth. This story is but one episode in the long process of my spiritual cultivation.

Some years after my initial exploration of the nature of true mind, I remarked to my father, "I have discovered that the true mind is not the colorful construction of all religions. Nor is it the atmosphere created by the many different churches and temples. Neither is it the different doctrines and rituals practiced in various ceremonies and celebrations. These practices are just various expressions of human custom and are not the ultimate, immutable truth. None of them has any solution to the question of life and death; they are merely useless decorations for the plain process of human life and death. Not one of them is the result of the discovery of truth. They serve only as psychological coverings or artistic beautification to human disappointment and despair. Beneath all these different forms of entertainment, these ornamental measures, lies utter impoverishment and helplessness. Such religious practices go against the true mind. To follow a religion is to proceed in the opposite direction of the true mind."

I paused for approval from my father. He responded, "What you say is not the practice of the true mind. The practice of the true mind is not the practice of criticism. In all the examples you mentioned, there is the opportunity for the important practice of non-bewilderment within any confused situation. In other words, the practice of true mind as an accurate response on these occasions is the practice of clarity. The true mind is responsive, but does not lose its clarity because of its own responsiveness."

At that particular moment I felt I had received the key and I expressed my gladness and good understanding. I said, "Truly, truly, though the criticism was perceived through my achieved clarity, I separate my mind from the clarity when I criticize. Knowledge is something that has already been established, while clarity is the unformed, true mind. It can be compared with the relationship of the sky and clouds, knowledge being the clouds which hinder the clarity of the sky. From now on, I shall keep myself to the fundamental virtue of mind-clarity without deviation or separation by established knowledge or emotion."

My father responded, "Be careful, son. Clarity is only one virtue of the true mind. There are still equally important practices of the true mind, such as the practice of sincerity, the practice of freedom from temptation, the practice of the Mind of Non-Evasion In Any Moment, the practice of the Mind of Composure and Peace, the practice of the Mind of Non-Dissipation, the practice of Dispassion, the practice of the Unattached Mind, the practice of the Impartial Mind and the practice of the Mind of Harmony, among many other virtues. These are all important in attaining clarity of the mind.

"Among all virtues of the mind, only clarity and sincerity are basic powers of the true mind. Neither can be separated

from the other. To have sincerity without clarity is foolish.
To have clarity without sincerity is to be a disinterested
bystander of worldly people and matters. Any single
virtuous practice is a rigid or dogmatic practice. Obviously
this is not the way to reach Tao.

"Also, be sure that a specific virtue is not neglected
when facing a specific circumstance, otherwise you will lose
the correct response of the true mind. Tao is the totality.
Tao cannot be put into partial practice. The practice of a
single virtue has helped some people earn fame as a so-
called saint, but in reality this is using the entire being to
fulfill what is a partial expression of life. This is why
ordinary religious people are in danger of losing the view of
the wholeness of life. This is one extreme. On the opposite
side, ordinary non-religious people use their entire being to
fulfill a single desire or emotional attachment. This is
another extreme. Thus, cultivating the wholeness of life is
the complete development of an individual human being. If
one has reached an understanding of the wholeness of life,
one can see that many past religious leaders and saints died
before they had developed themselves completely. In other
words, they died for the sake of only one part of their
integral being. As Heavenly models, this was misleading
and actually a serious matter of personal underdevelopment. They set incomplete examples which have misled
those who followed. The highest examples of complete
virtue are not even recognized by most people since the
leader with complete, absolute virtue works quietly and
subtly. When he has accomplished his task and completed
his duty, people say: 'It is we ourselves who have made it
so.' Leaders who have plain good virtue attract followers
who like to be with them and who respect and honor them.
The forceful leader creates a strong emotional response
among people. Among of these virtuous beings, only the
first is the one we follow with complete willingness!"

At this moment, my previous enlightenment was revealed in all its shallowness. I struggled with my young
pride and said, "Now I understand that the true mind is the
balanced mind. The true mind is the integral mind. The
true mind is the crystal clear mind. The true mind is the

transcendental mind, and the true mind is the natural, unspoiled mind. It contains all positive virtues. The fragmentary insistence on one or a few chosen virtues is dangerous. Now I truly understand what the ancestors said: 'Rigid practice is the thief and robber of the way of the true mind."

My father said: "Well, even I can agree that now you have something. The mind is part of our entire being. The mind is the latecomer of our life being. In our lives, there are some things which are more fundamental than the mind. The work you did with your mind was to remove the poisons of the vulgar mind. There are not many more secrets of the mind. The secret of life is chi, which precedes all human life and continues to exist after the human flesh-life has transformed. After studying the game of the mystery of the mind comes the more important cultivation of chi. One who only learns the mind may speak better, but achieving real spiritual growth is another matter. Herein lies the importance of cultivating chi."

Chapter 45

No Idolization

Among the undeveloped, "idolization" is often used to assemble people. However, in cultivating spiritual growth, "idolization" can be an obstacle if it is incorrectly applied. The following gives instruction and guidance as to its influence in spiritual matters.

> "Confucianism is my garment,
> Buddhism is my cane, and
> Taoism is my sandal."

This "three-in-one" spiritual movement was the actual response of a vast number of Chinese people in the Tang Dynasty (628-906 A.D.) to the rise of Buddhism, which prospered because of the support of the royal court and thus became the third most important element in Chinese cultural life. Most Chinese scholars accepted this new cultural condition by considering Confucianism, Taoism and Buddhism as the three legs of a cauldron. In ancient Chinese symbology, the Cauldron represents unification, thus Confucianism, Taoism and Buddhism became the harmonizing forces in the lives of Chinese people.

My family's spiritual focus did support the work of cultural integration in order to help ourselves and help the awakening of all people. Our real spiritual foundation was the three classics of mysticism 三玄 , the *Book of Changes*, the *Tao Teh Ching* by Lao Tzu and the book of *Chuang Tzu*, which expresses the principles of balance, symmetry, evenness, equality and harmony. Plus, there were three other books considered as the three great treasures of Taoist heritage 三 十墳 . They are Fu Shi's *I Ching*, the Yellow Emperor's *Internal Book* (also called *The Yellow Emperor's Classic of Internal Medicine?) and* Shen Nung's *Herb Book*. These are what are greatly appreciated.

Sometimes the *Book of Changes* is considered mystical because its principles are expressed with signs instead of words. Many scholars have been perplexed by the signs of this book's ancient metaphors and concise language. The key to the *Book of Changes* is to maintain balance in all situations involving change. With such eminent guidance for life and culture, it is not unusual that Chinese scholars would adopt an attitude of harmonization amid the cultural conflicts of their time.

Under the high principles of the *Book of Changes*, these three religions of Buddhism, Confucianism and Taoism functioned mainly as different sources of education for the majority of Chinese people. Though each appeared independent of the other, each actually absorbed the other over the course of time. In our present generation, a careful scholar would have no difficulty discovering that present-day Confucianism absorbed Taoism, Taoism absorbed Confucianism and Buddhism combined with religious Taoism.

Hermetic Taoism unavoidably responded to the new situation by adopting a principle of "balanced cultivation," which meant keeping conceptual training on a level with spiritual training. After the Tang Dynasty, some ancient leaders from the Taoist tradition actually became the practical leaders of this new spiritual integration, with achievements that have been recorded throughout history.

My father was in his late years when I was born; thus, when I was in my teens and began to know and understand things, my father had already achieved spiritual maturity and could enjoy his high achievement. I greatly benefitted by the broad background he provided me.

The three lines which begin this chapter were an inspiration to me. I wrote them on a piece of paper and put them on the wall of my study. The words happened to be overheard by one of my father's serious friends who was most appreciative of them. This man shared the words with all his friends because they actually expressed the harmonizing attitude of Chinese people: they adopted Confucianism as their social and family mode; they adopted Buddhism as their emotional support; and they practiced Taoism in their practical life.

On one occasion I met my father's highly developed friend and he remarked: "I heard you that wrote: 'Confucianism is my garment, Buddhism is my cane, and

Taoism is my sandal.' At your age, how much can you know about Confucianism, Buddhism and Taoism? Now, you must tell me. If your answer does not meet with my satisfaction, I will not let you go home. I shall keep you here in my study to finish reading my many years' collection of good books."

My answer was: "You asked about my garment; please ask the tailor. You asked about my cane; please ask the cane-maker. And you asked about my sandal; please ask the shoe-maker."

He seemed surprised and pleased. After a moment he exclaimed: "Your answer is unbelievable! If it were from the mouth of an aged master, it would be meaningful, but it came from a young boy like you. However hard it is to believe, I am convinced. A father tiger never gives birth to a dog son."

He then asked his family to come into the living room to meet me. Now I could leave with a light heart. However, this matter was not yet over. He later repeated our dialogue to his good friends. With bewilderment and skepticism, this group of friends met to discuss the matter and, wishing to discover the truth about me, invited me to their meeting. I sat quietly among all these elders of my father's spiritual kingdom.

While everybody was leisurely sipping their tea, the chair elder said to me: "We heard of Mr. Lin's profound experience with you. He told us about your conversation and gave you a high evaluation for spiritual achievement. We have hoped for someone in the younger generation to be able to do something for the world, but this is not something that can be expected of a particular person without the real approval of the Divine Realm. Spirituality has its own unmistaken standard of what is true and not true. Now we would like to see for ourselves how you present the tradition in front of us, since you say: 'Confucianism is your garment, Buddhism is your cane, and Taoism is your sandal.'

"We are not concerned with how much you have read about Confucianism or Buddhism, or even how much you know about Taoism. What we would like to know is that if Confucianism is the garment, Buddhism is the cane, and

Taoism is the sandal, then who is the user? Now tell us, who is the true one who dresses himself in the garment, holds the cane, and wears the sandal? This is all we need to know. It is a rule that you not hesitate in answering the question."

"The awakened Chinese people," was my answer.

Everybody seemed quite satisfied, but the examination continued. "What do you mean by the awakened Chinese people?"

"Six thousand years ago there were no teachings of Confucianism, Buddhism and probably none of Taoism either. Furthermore, those people did not consider themselves as "Chinese" people who were different from other people. People such as they are the ones who truly use and enjoy all of these teachings. Clothing should be made to fit the people; people should not be made to fit the clothing."

Their level of interest seemed to be increasing, thus the questioning continued.

"Why do you specify the 'awakened' Chinese people and not all the people of China and the rest of the world?"

"This is the level the 'awakened' Chinese people have reached. When all the people of the world reach this same level, freedom from religious and philosophical conflicts can be realized and the harmonization of the human spirit can be reached."

"You said that six thousand years ago, there were no teachings of Confucianism, Buddhism, nor were there written words of Taoism, and that the people of China did not know they were "Chinese." And that people such as those are the ones who truly use and enjoy all of these teachings. And furthermore that clothing should be made to fit the people; people should not be made to fit the clothing.' Exactly how much of this is your own contribution?"

"I do not claim original credit for this point of view. Rebellious people also use these words, but what they say has no true spiritual value. My spiritual value was obtained from serious cultivation, thus I do not speak out of rebellious ignorance. From spiritual achievement I am able to reach the truth. I value the healthy spiritual education that the past human race developed. I deny anything which can be an obstruction in reaching the truth."

"Wait a moment," one of them exclaimed, "this is the point we really need to know. Now, what is the truth you have reached, and by what books were you inspired? Quickly, tell us!"

In this room was a table on which were many different important books and translations of world religions. At this moment I was inspired and stacked all the books into one pile as a stool and sat on them. Someone then passed me one copy of Lao Tzu and one copy of Chuang Tzu, and said: "Take these also, to make you sit higher." When I refused, he demanded the reason.

I answered: "I know what is beneath me, and what is not beneath me."

"That is an evasive answer. What is your real answer?" he demanded.

"In response to your demand, I can see you are worried that I idolize these books as my innermost precious spiritual treasure. I would ask that you recognize that I have not idolized anything. I earnestly give recognition to Lao Tzu, the source of my spiritual nursing, and to Chuang Tzu, who postulated that even the intimate truth - Tao, the great true Oneness - cannot be idolized. Thus, allow me not to be an ungrateful student and friend."

One of the elders then slowly explained the following to me: "This point is the most important heritage of our spiritual family. Though it is already clear to you, it is absolutely necessary that it be made explicit. It must never become confused or mixed up. The spiritual practice of some traditions of the world is to deny the idolization of anything.   But as a consequence, one consciously or unconsciously begins to idolize oneself instead. This is a practice of shallowness and rigidity and is a spiritual dead end. Some spiritual traditions deny all nameable things, yet affirm 'oneself' or the 'self,' thus they have reached nowhere. The one who follows the true path knows that everything in the universe is already oneself. There is nothing that can be denied without 'self,' nor is there anything that can be affirmed as 'self.' If everything is denied, then the 'self' is affirmed. If the 'self' is denied, then who is the one making the denial? None of them has reached the breakthrough of the two-sided spiritual practice of yin and yang. In other words, they have not reached spiritual unity.

"In our spiritual family ('family' meaning the followers of the true path), when we deny the idolization of anything, our purpose is not to affirm 'self' but to present the wholeness of Tao, which is already an integration of everything, including the 'self.' This is the reason Tao is indefinable. Total harmony and spiritual unity can be achieved when idolization of all things is removed. This is not accomplished with a negative spirit, as in other traditions, but it is achieved by following a balanced and harmonized path which leads to Tao. Tao is the integrity, the wholeness, of the origin. Thus we do not accept any name for the unspoiled naturalness of the great reality of the oneness. As you know, this is how your father guided all of us."

Finally, they seemed to have reached an understanding that they need not trouble me with further questions. Spiritually I had almost reached their level. Then, the atmosphere of the meeting changed again. Another elder asked: "We feel satisfied with the growth of your positive spirit. On a practical level, it can be interpreted as: no life needs to be sacrificed, nor wars fought for religious reasons or conceptual conflicts. To illustrate, the common people of China eat swine; however, the Chinese Islams do not. There were two villages in the western region of China. One village raised and ate swine, while the Islamic village did not. This incident was enough to cause a great battle between the two villages. This is a simple example of exaggerating a 'principle' and then using it as justification for conflict.

"Another example of this principle from history was the Crusades. What did people who participated in those persecutions accomplish except exaltation of religious prejudice?"

Another elder then said: "The real problem is not the pervasion of religious prejudice, it is the darkness of people's minds. Thus, they find excuses to fight over religious teachings. There is no way to correct this except by the spiritual development of the entire world. Achieved people know the 'true mind' and do not fall prey to idolization of religious leaders or doctrines.

"When one holds tightly to a concept, clarity is lost. If clarity is lost, the situation can never be rightfully handled. Having a 'leader' is no longer a good concept because emotions have now become the 'ruler.' Even if a good idea is presented, by idolizing it - putting it into a rigid mold - its connection with the original truthfulness is lost and much harm can undoubtedly be caused.

"For example, in one of our big cities, there was a young girl who wanted to marry a boy with a completely different culture and religion than hers. Her parents were opposed on the principle that marriage alone would be difficult for two young people, but to bridge two entirely different worlds of cultural and religious upbringing would be an impossible task. They considered this relationship to be an especially bad match because of their strong attachment to their own religion and they feared that such a marriage could dilute the religious beliefs of the next generation.

"The boy and girl were idealistically in love and believed they could transcend their cultural differences and find a common ground. The influence of the discouraging parents on both sides, however, strongly affected the couple and eventually the young lovers killed themselves.

"Another example is one's love for nation. Such a situation is similar to one's idealistic love for a child, in that emotions dominate; thus, one's ability to be clear and right-minded is lost. The issue of politics is similar to the issue of emotions in that both are the real reasons behind the actions which affect most people."

After further discussion, the eldest member made his stately conclusion and directed it towards me: "It will not be far in the future when darkness will over-power this part of the world. You are the one who will be able to provide the light. If our material possessions and anything else can be preserved, and if you need them, they will all be at your command. We also realize this could be our wishful thinking; however, this is the way for us to express our concern and support in awakening the entire world toward spiritual maturity without creating conflicts by idolizing spiritual images or human authorities. When people are not truly developed spiritually, power can make them mad. Power can be useful in helping to accomplish great virtuous merits when entrusted to the hands of virtuous world leaders."

When he finished talking, he asked me to read a chapter of Lao Tzu and said, "After reading, you may go."

This is what I read:

> "When people of the world live in accordance
>   with the way of universal harmonization,
>   horses are used for agricultural purposes.
>
> "When people of the world do not live in accordance
>   with the way of universal harmonization,
>   then horses and even pregnant mares
>   are driven to the battlefield and bred there.
>
> "There is no greater calamity for a nation,
>   as well as for an individual,
>   than not to find one's own sufficiency
>   through peaceful measures.
>
> "There is no greater mistake for a nation,
>   as well as for an individual,
>   than to be covetous of more and more
>   goods of another,
>   and thus become involved in contention."
>   (Chapter 46 of the Tao Teh Ching)

Chapter 46

The Immortal Subtle Body is Within You

The timeless body of a superman was originally ours to have, but we destroyed ourselves with uncontrolled passions and lust. In our desire for wealth, fame and sensual love, we drowned.

Though we live a hundred years, time will pass quickly - empty pursuits will see to that. If our lives are conducted like a sloppily-run business, we will end our years with nothing.

Thus, always keep your mind empty, like the great space of the universe. Do not obstruct the smooth course of waters and clouds. Just as waters flow smooth and free, so should the mind be kept clear of sticky impediments.

Keep the same innocence inside as out. This is the way to wholeness. It is within you, the immortal, spiritual, subtle body. Do not mistakenly go begging and searching outside for it.

The road to becoming a Shien is clearly marked. It is your impatience and desires that blind your spiritual eyes. If you remove all covers and obstacles right here and now, you will know the origin of your life. A long pilgrimage is not necessary to find your source. If you get sidetracked on an evil path, try though you may to achieve self-cultivation, you will be moving against the Tao. Stay whole, stay clean, stay firm - and in one moment you can experience everything of Tao and become an adored child of Heaven.

Chapter 47

The Mystical Change of the Person Who Succeeds in Connecting his Energy with the Subtle, Divine Energy of the Universe

---

One is no longer tempted by former bad habits, nor does one chase after worldly pleasures. Old physical maladies gradually and completely disappear. The mind is right, and the body reflects one's righteousness.

One stands firmly on one's own two feet. Deep calm pervades one's internal and external atmosphere. One finds one has both the time and the energy to accomplish any task. One purifies oneself and is at peace with one's environment. One never becomes violent and has untiring patience with one's fellow beings. One is worry-free and always has a joyful heart. One is never jealous of another's prominence nor greedy for the possessions prized by others. One has no ambition to live a vain or luxurious life.

Because one eats simply, one maintains serenity. One keeps one's physical desire subdued and one's virtue high. One develops true and deep knowledge, dissolves all obstacles, and extends oneself to meet the straight and eternal Way. Thus, one experiences uncritically that concepts of life and death are merely the ebb and flow of the eternal breath of Tao.

One dissolves one's ego and with it all internal and external conflicts. One does not seek one's own longevity or personal happiness, nor does one struggle to hold onto material things. One does not use the speakable as truth to suppress those who are silent. One has no desire to go beyond one's means or ability. In one's pure mind, one holds no illusions or strange thinking.

One nurtures a firm character through selfless giving and self-oblivion, never emphasizes what one does that is right, nor claim credit for one's undertakings. One knows things thoroughly from beginning to end. Virtuously, one knows there are certain things one will never do.

One avoids involvement in contests for worldly profit or glory. One is amiable and useful. One embodies harmonious equilibrium and creative appropriateness. One enjoys ease, both internally and externally. One strives only to surpass one's own virtue. One obeys the universal Spirit in order to evolve higher. Before touching the formed, one rests in the unformed. One enlightens oneself and never tires of awakening the world.

Chapter 48

Purity of Mind

When the full moon arrives in the heights of the sky,
a breeze blows over the water.
I believe there are not many
who know the taste of purity.

-poem by a nature poet of the Chin Dynasty (265-420 A.D.)

A pond of half an acre
is like a mirror reflecting the sky.
From high in the sky often comes
the shadow of flying clouds,
making their visit then quickly passing.
How can I attain such purity?
Because within me there is a living fountain.

-poem by a philosopher of the Sung Dynasty (960-1279 A.D.)

These are two poems my father brushed in red ink on Chinese bamboo paper. When I was five, he made me copy his written characters in black ink, as my initiation into ancient Chinese cultural life. In my time, pre-school education was given to children by their parents. I was not special. However, the material my father adopted was different from what other families used, and it was this which was engraved upon my innocent heart.

It is the true knowledge of all developed people that no life can be free from troubles, but the mind can be trouble-free after spiritual achievement. The unaffected mind is often illustrated by analogy with the sky and clouds. The passions or emotions with which people react to troubles are like the clouds, or the "substance" of the mind. The true mind, which can take the troubles and reactions and yet remain unchanging, is like the sky.

Various reactions to the occurrence of "clouds" covering the "sky" - i.e., the passions, emotions, or pain which overcome the mind - developed into different attitudes or modes or responses toward the problem. An intellectual would conclude that since it is the "clouds" that cause the trouble, it is the "clouds" that need to be dispersed. In the view of some Buddhist teachings, it is the "sky" which should be destroyed since it is the canvas on which trouble can occur. Most other religions invite thieves to catch thieves. They chase thieves away, but invite new ones to come. This is simply substituting an artificial faith or a strong image to support the falseness of the reacting mind.

In contrast, Taoists apply the principle of naturalness, leaving the "sky" as the "sky" and distinguishing it from the "clouds" which come and go and which can therefore never really affect the vastness and profundity of the "sky," that is to say, the true mind.

Intellectualizing or analyzing the clouds, or "tearing down the sky" (denouncing the mind completely as the way of solving all problems at once), or using thieves to govern thieves, are all ways of responding to the same phenomena. However, in Taoist understanding, the "clouds" enable the beauty of the sky to be appreciated, and the beauty of the "sky" is what gives significance to the "clouds."

On a conscious level, it is easy to see the association of "clouds" and "sky" with pain and the mind which experiences pain. When one appears to exist, the other is also present. Balance should always exist as the normal relationship between the mind and its feelings. The elementary practice of the true, unaffected mind can help one reach the true path. For a balanced mind there is nothing to talk about; for an excited mind, there is always much to discuss. To maintain quiet-mindedness is an achievement, although it is not a rigid demand in Taoism. Nothing can be rigidly practiced in Taoism, because it is not a dogmatic religion.

Once a man whose life had been full of misery came to seek guidance from my father. In order to retreat from his previous worldly life, he had gone to live in a temple in the mountains. Usually, a visitor who had traveled a long way would stay with us for several days. My father received this guest in our garden. As a pupil and attendant of my father, I could see from our guest's eyes, eyebrows, and overall face that although he had retreated from the troubled world, his mind had not completely retreated from his past troubles. During this meeting my father offered him no guidance; instead, my father was more involved in watching a young cat chase a butterfly and its shadow around a flower bush. The butterfly flew here and there, lower and higher, nimble and elusively, while the young cat anxiously tried to catch it. My father's involvement with this scene naturally directed our attention to the cat. The butterfly now flew away, but just as the cat began to relax, it flew back again. This repeated challenge and provocation made the cat even more intent in its desire to catch the butterfly. "To catch it" became the sole necessity of the cat, because it seemed the cat would not admit failure, as I could understand through my own excited blood flow.

Presently, my father had to leave to take care of a patient, and the guest and I were alone in the garden. Without moving our eyes away from the scene of the cat and the butterfly, he asked me, "What does your father teach you now?"

"He asks me to recite the ancient medical books."

"Medicine has no Tao," he commented, and continued, "Start early. Do not learn the Tao as late as I do. My life was full of events. Now my mind is full of misery. My life was eroded by all those unworthy experiences. What you cultivate in one day now may take me long years to achieve."

"My father once told me, 'The ancient medicine is Tao in a narrow way of practice. Tao is medicine in the broad way of practice. Other than the healing effects of Tao as medicine, our tradition has little to offer the ordinary world.'"

My answer astonished him. Just then, the cat suddenly jumped to catch the butterfly, which barely escaped.

After we both recovered from the tension created by watching the great chase, he retorted: "If the Tao is medicine, there should be no incurable disease. If this is so, then why has all my family died? As you can see, many people have died from disease."

His retort made me impatient. I was busy taking sides in the great chase. Sometimes I took the side of the cat, and other times, the butterfly. I always silently "hurried" the one who moved more slowly. At the same time, I was anxious about the "real catch."

Then I exclaimed, "My father said that there is no incurable disease. There are only incurable people."

"Ah!" was his only utterance. I was not sure if his "ah" was aimed at me, at the danger of the butterfly, or at the pathetic expression of the cat's failure. I decided his "ah" was for me, not fully understanding what he meant.

I continued: "Healers are for general diseases, but a person must take responsibility himself for the important matters in his life. He is the one who must live the life he has molded. If he plays the destroyer of his life and then asks others to play the rescuer, can anything be achieved?"

"Ah! Ah!" was the sound he made, but his bodily posture sank.

I continued, "Taoist cultivation, as I know it, is to be self-healing or self-regulating at the fundamental level. Self-development and self-achievement are at an advanced level. However, each step must be taken with good spirit and accomplished by oneself. Only when the dough is ready should the yeast be applied. Otherwise, it is a waste to make a long journey to see any great master."

This time he made no response at all. Instead, he slowly stood up and picked up his bag, moved his eyes from the still active cat and turned his face. He began with a sigh, then slowly and with integrity said: "I have received medicine from your venerable family. I did not waste my trip. After some years, I shall return to express my gratitude if I have proved I am worthy." Then he bowed and left.

Years later, during the great invasion and bombing, people who lived in the cities or important towns left because of "the tension of the times," as the Chinese people called it. I was sent to a temple in the mountains. I was greeted there by the keeper, with whom I felt some familiarity and was asked to take a seat in the main hall. He then sublimely saluted me in a traditional way, took from his big sleeve a piece of rice paper that was folded into a square, and handed it to me. I opened the paper which contained a neatly written poem:

"Worldly life is but a cat
endlessly chasing the shadow of a butterfly.
Nothing is real.
Long ago I stopped playing the cat's game.
The long ignorant one finally becomes a spiritual tiger
in the secluded mountain."

Suddenly, I recalled who he was and we had a good laugh. I enjoyed the several weeks of my stay there. Besides having the good energy of the mountain, I also had the company of a spiritually developed one.

Not long ago, one of my American students asked the meaning of the "Heavenly Gate" referred to in Chapter 10 of the *Tao Teh Ching.* At the same time, someone else asked the meaning of "destiny." I immediately recalled this story and gave my answer for the meaning of the "Heavenly Gate" as follows:

When the Subtle Gate opens, one receives life; when it closes, one's life is transformed. The Subtle Gate is continually opening and closing; therefore, one's destiny is continually changing.

The opportunity arises for one to receive life when the Subtle Gate opens widely. When one's star looks dark, one may believe that the Subtle Gate leaves only a "narrow pass" for him, but how many "narrow passes" or critical moments occur in one's life? Are such moments also met by others? Actually, because of one's own tension and restlessness, one nervously and mistakenly pulls the invisible string to hasten the closing and opening of the "Subtle Gate," thus disregarding the natural rhythm of life.

The Subtle Door is a door of no door, a gate of no gate. It is the constantly changing level of the mind which separates the reality of the continuous transformability of our destiny from the unsentimental cycle of life. The feelable destiny and other emotions and passions are all misbelief of our life. The tensions of the mind breed such misbeliefs. Misconceptions or incorrect feelings build a self-deceptive psychological life.

Chapter 49

The Work of Awakening

Language awakens the minds of people, chi awakens the chi of people. The world needs both a truly awakening language and a truly awakening energy.

There is nothing more significant than for one to stay awake. There is also nothing more meaningful than to awaken others. The awakened one maintains wholeness and constant balance. He does not participate in any mob movements, nor does he give up the world. He lives among worldly people without being discouraged by their ignorance, stubbornness and aggression. He maintains his awakened nature.

By what method did he achieve himself? By what method will he help others? What is the reality of awakening in the natural and supernatural Taoist tradition?

Some Taoist secret methods of spiritual achievement are only allowed to be passed down to three human beings every seven hundred years. Others are only allowed to be passed on to one human being every thousand years. These methods support a person's high achievement. To limit the spreading of such secret methods, there are different Heavenly prohibitions accompanying different levels of achievement. When I look at the misguided direction of the general human culture, I wish Heaven would allow us to remove all these prohibitions. If the truth of life and of universal formation were totally revealed to all, would this not end all arguments and wars among people, and would this not be a beautiful thing?

I have often asked myself: Should I risk breaking the Heavenly prohibitions in revealing the general sacred truths for the purpose of correcting the improper educational guidance in schools and society? Should I tell people that the first important objective in their education is to recognize their own true nature? Can I tell people that they have a divine nature, or should I just tell them that human nature is already semi-godly with the potential of restoring its "other-half" - its divine nature? Can I show the truth, through self-cultivation, of how a human being can give birth to a spirit which can further one's visible life? Can I show the truth that, through cultivation, one human life can give birth to numerous spiritual beings? Can I reveal the truth that through correct cultivation, the essence of each organ in the human body can transform into a "womb" for a spiritual baby, which can later become independent in the universe with complete senses and capabilities? Can I tell people that their own spiritual development directly determines the quality, capability, virtue and destination of the spirit which could be born from them?

Have I enabled people to see the value of the balanced way: that neither the narrow practice of religion nor the self-indulgence of the secular way is correctly centered? Can people, through my work, understand that the paths of idealism and materialism are both one-sided and miss the mark? Can I tell the world's people the truth of life so that they may re-evaluate and readjust all the school books which have already gone astray by their partial vision from the truth of life and of the universe?

Why must spiritual truth be limited to certain individuals? Why cannot spiritual truth become public education? Why does spiritual achievement become a domain which only a few specially developed people can share and enjoy?

I often ask myself such questions. In order to soothe my burning compassion for my fellow people of the world, I remind myself of the following.

In my own knowledge of spiritual growth, if the secret gate were suddenly opened to an ordinary man or woman, this person would surely become mad. One's mental capacity is not prepared for this spiritual achievement. Thus, the Heavenly prohibition can be regarded with the clear understanding that it is actually Heaven's protection. This protection is not only for an individual who is interested in learning, but is also a protection for others who might immaturely practice what they have learned.

The incorrect knowledge system of the ordinary world is part of the process of human growth. Children ask for cookies and toys, not truth. In the same manner, intellectual knowledge systems of human life are the toys which most people play with in their life. The truth of life is simple and clear. If people wake up, they can see it.

There are three main obstacles which serve as poisons and thus prohibit people from seeing the truth: ignorance, stubbornness and aggression. How can an achieved one help? If the achieved one is passive towards these people, then he will give up the world to live in seclusion. If he is active and responds to the world's people, his warmth gathers their ignorance, stubbornness and aggression to himself. Hundreds of times, he may tell himself to leave, but where can he go? Where are there people of no darkness, no obstinacy and no aggression? Should he retreat to become a hermit, as did the ancient ones who traversed the Silent Way? The demands of their generation were much different from this one. If he should want to stop after giving a class, a talk, or writing a book, there always comes the same response from the Old Master:

> Do it without anticipation.
> Do it without assertiveness.
> Do it without self.

A hundred times he may answer the Old Master, "It is no fun!" But he may always answer himself, "Is there anything more fun than awakening people? One must keep oneself wholly and constantly awakening!"

Language awakens the minds of people. Chi awakens the chi of people. The world needs more than just awakening energy and awakening language.

Chapter 50

No Separation

The spiritual application of the hexagram Ting, Harmonization/Balance ☲☴ , is illustrated by the following story.

As a young boy, I esteemed enlightenment above all else. I knew there were many things of high spiritual value to be learned in my tradition, but I nonetheless thought of enlightenment as the "express train" which could take me directly to the subtle origin of all lives, as well as to the six breakthroughs, the milestones of self-development, which would mark my high spiritual capability and free me from further dependency on other spiritual beings.

Until I was in my late forties, the attainment of such enlightenment and breakthroughs were my highest achievements. Naturally, these achievements made my life and work more effective, whether in healing or teaching, but I realized there was more to learn.

For an enlightened one, the world is the altar on which he offers his cultivation. One who is enlightened is no longer spiritually connected to people on a common, undeveloped level. An enlightened one, returning to the people of the world, is like a well-disciplined child going outside to play in the "mud." Regardless of how clean he was before going outside, he will get at least somewhat dirty, yet return to the world he must. As a gift to humanity and as the virtuous realization of his own being, an enlightened one must fulfill his natural and supernatural responsibilities. (Just as the sun, moon and stars in the vast sky are the sources of illumination for an entirely dark world, how could people live in darkness without the light of a developed one?)

Even though the enlightened one has reached the level of spiritual achievement, the fact remains that the world is not naturally morally-ordered. Therefore, an achieved one must continue to safeguard his offering from the harm of evil when extending his being to the world. What one has, after achieving enlightenment and the six breakthroughs, is the purified, responsive yang energy of a human being. Thus, such a one needs even more spiritual protection from the shadow realm of evil spirits and evil people. Even with pure yang energy, without further development through the real divine method, without learning how to protect oneself from being used as a tool of evil ghosts, one is still vulnerable, or sometimes even more vulnerable, to spiritual attack from the inferior world. People who suddenly become possessed have been attacked because they relinquished their self-control and rational behavior. Even though such evil is the product of undevelopment, it may still cause much harm. The offensive evil cannot be punished, and the traditional, righteous spiritual power cannot be extended over the evil ones. Although enlightenment has been achieved, spiritual dominance is still foreign.

I realized that, although I had experienced many high spiritual peaks, my cultivation was still incomplete. When enlightenment carried me from darkness to the light and from wrong to right, its function was accomplished. However, lightness and rightness are still within the relative realm. Thus, enlightenment is really just the beginning of developing oneself beyond the level of duality. Though the function of enlightenment is to improve one's consciousness and fundamental concepts, it still does not reach the reality of the real spiritual beings.

You might well ask: what is a real spirit, and what is the real immortal realm? What is the connection of one's spiritual being with the immortal realm? Such questions had been at the center of my ancestors' spiritual endeavors, and now they were mine. I realized that up to this point, I had been unrealistic, achieving myself mostly through idealistic efforts. As I now discovered in my cultivation, I was only partially developed, with what is expressible only on a human level.

In order to fill the gap that existed between the spiritual realm and a human being with a flesh body, I decided to once again become a beginner and to learn the real divine practices of my tradition and become thoroughly trained in the details of the ancient methods outlined by Pao Pu Tzu.

At first, my efforts were concentrated on making contact with a particular Heavenly being. Then I developed my connection to the divine ones with special spiritual functions. Finally, I worked on the total, unifying spiritualization of my own being. The main harvest of my advanced spiritual cultivation, which began in my late forties, was to end the separation between universal beings, my spiritual being, and my human being. This reunion can also be expressed as a metaphor: "The body is an empire, while the universe is a body."

Now, anywhere I go and every place I stay, I meet spiritual beings of good will, joyful communication and great harmony. What a truly supernatural privilege to enjoy the reality of no separation.

Chapter 51

Stay with the Unshaken Fundamental Path of Tao

According to the generally accepted philosophical view, the law of cause and effect is supreme. Nothing is excluded from it. All things are the product of a cause or an effect. However, Tao, the path of all, takes another view. To what cause does the origin of Tao belong since it originates itself? Therefore, Tao is above the law of cause and effect.

One way to put it is that Tao itself is the law - it is self-natured. Tao is the first nature of the universe, of divinity, of matter and of humankind. While other things have a second or even a third nature, Tao has only one absolute nature. Tao is all nature. It is the first principle which is completely beyond reason. Therefore, to look for Tao by using reason or thought is like climbing a tree in search of fish eggs.

In Tao, all causes and all effects merge into oneness. There is no more confrontation between what is the cause and what is the effect. Because a cause is no more to become a cause and an effect is no more an effect. They fulfill the complete Tai Chi; yin and yang embrace each other like .

Chapter 52

Virtue

Build a house of Tao on a foundation of virtue.
With virtue there is union.
Subtle power comes not just from within ourselves,
but from Heaven, Earth and all living things
working positively through us.
The mind embraces all positive virtues.
Without being separate, you contribute to all things,
creating a solid immortality with the whole universe.
Strengthen your virtues and become
forever, naturally firm, beyond decay.

Obediently follow the great Tao with a single mind
and all anxieties will fall away.
The inferior mind is the origin
of all trouble and sickness.
To treat your illness, first treat your mind.
As the impure mind becomes active,
all manner of negative obstacles arise.
As the mind calms, shadows and hardships disappear.
A harmonious mind breeds no disease.
Pride and self-neglect both breed imbalance.
To know the cause is to know the cure.

Do not think of Tao as a theoretical arrangement.
The improvement of your life
depends on honest self-cultivation.
Cultivate the awareness that obstacles are impurities.
Melt through your mental formations
to the eternal reality.
Unite with the final truth.
Treat your mind and body with your mind and body.
Trace differences back to their origin.
Through the truest cultivation,
discipline, proof and gain,
become the son or daughter
of the highest Heavenly family.

Chapter 53

The Sacred Method

The key to Tao cultivation lies in the eyes.
The eyes gather color and form which,
*   when too active, hinder cultivation*
*   and drain energy.*

Hold all six gates serene and pure.
Remove all distraction from the ears and eyes
*   to keep your energy full and your spirit whole.*
Keep the mind from wandering.
The subtle body is like nature and Heaven.
It receives all and holds nothing.

The origin of suffering lies in the body of flesh.
Make it the altar of self-cultivation.
Trickery and deceit do not benefit the body.
What may seem good for your body
*   may damage your mind,*
*   and a damaged mind holds no home for the soul.*

Adding a title to your name,
*   or a decoration to your personality,*
*   is not the way of a whole being.*
True benefit is found in the efforts
*   of your own deep soul.*
Real benefit is not found in social reputation.
True gain is measured deep within yourself.
For the Sacred Method to be real
*   and practical in the realm of life,*
*   to be a Heavenly whole being, a Shien,*
*   one must have deep spiritual roots.*

Choosing an heir to the Sacred Way
*   must be done with care.*
This is not the same as doing favors
*   for the whole world.*
Love and value the Sacred Method.

Do not carelessly throw it away.
Observe those with true spiritual affinity
  for the way of eternity
  and those without.
The Grand Masters of the Sacred Method
  bid us again and again
  to fully protect this treasure
  in a cautious way.

Chapter 54

No Bondage

After the good conditions of life are met - health, finances, security, a solid relationship, a good living environment, etc. - and one decides to raise children, one needs to have a clear understanding of this commitment. If one becomes a mother or a father and lives in a normal society with a normal pattern of life, then twenty-five years of self-sacrifice must be anticipated.

The traditional purpose and benefit of marriage is to raise children. In order to provide psychological security and healthy growth for the young, a binding marriage is practical. Aside from this particular purpose, a binding marriage is harmful, especially for natural spiritual cultivation. If the marriage is not a case of feeding each other the three poisons (ignorance, stubbornness, and aggressiveness), each person will still someday inevitably suffer the hidden erosion that comes about as the result of sharing the same bed or the same room.

Human beings are changeable animals. Of two people who are married in their early twenties, each may grow at a different rate, thus their personal development does not occur at the same pace. A match that was good ten or fifteen years earlier can seldom maintain this mutual pace and direction of development, and the distance between even a well-matched young couple widens, too. The harm of social, religious, or familial binding affects each person of the couple and, in particular, influences their moral responsibility to remain independent persons.

Love can be expressed in marriage, but it cannot be expressed in bondage. When one feels the bondage or obligation of a relationship, true love quickly dies.

All lovers dedicate themselves to each other with great respect and appreciate the love they receive. However, when they marry, their love often becomes an obligation and they come to take what love there was for granted. Thus, true love ceases to exist. If there is no true love, then how can such a relationship be called a marriage? It is a marriage with no "soul," a sad result of social custom and environmental conditioning.

A marital law which protects only one of the spouses is unjust. Marriage should be decided by the two people who love each other, and they should make the decision jointly. Divorce should be decided in the same manner. A good marriage cannot be established if one person does not love the other. Similarly, if the husband or wife no longer feels love, a divorce is in order. Any prohibition of divorce is inhuman, and anything inhuman is immoral. Alas, many immoral ways are inhumanities whose persecuting force has continued from the old, faded, insensitive customs of society or religion.

Improvement in married life can often be accomplished by taking a marriage "vacation." When a couple experiences difficulty, they can take a vacation from each other for a while instead of deciding to divorce as quickly as they married. If both parties recognize that the difficulty stems from emotional friction, then the true problem is not one of love, adjustments can be made accordingly. Thus, the marriage "vacation" offers a positive function. If divorce is the only answer, then a marriage vacation can also help each side see more clearly. No church, court of law or any other authority or outsider can determine the existence of a marriage between two people who are involved in love and life together. Other people can merely be witnesses to the decision.

If a divorce ensues, a husband should not take material profits from his wife. Likewise, the wife should not ask for money from her husband. But, if they so desire, they can offer each other a gift. As to distributing the wealth, if each party is working, then it should belong to the individual who created it. If only the husband has worked and is well off, and the wife has kept the home and is without a skill, the husband should make arrangements to adequately provide for her well-being. If there is equity in their life together, then the wealth should be equally divided. The children should belong to either one side or the other. A determination can be made as to who is more practically able to care for them.

A couple who has reached middle or old age after having been together for many years must maintain virtue in divorcing. The situation may be one in which the children are independent and the wife has no means or skill with which to support herself. Many women in this situation fear divorce, but the man should practice the virtue of a faithful old friend by offering to provide total or partial financial support for his wife for the rest of her life. The wife should practice her virtue of tolerance by not trying to deprive her husband of his natural rights. The fruits of their life can be shared equitably without creating deep worries for either side regarding old age.

In ancient Chinese society, marriage was not bondage. Marriages were based on organizing life to fulfill the practical responsibilities of maintaining their life, and rearing the next generation. The relationship between husband and wife did not emphasize emotional love. Their individual roles were based on mutual energy performance. While the wife devoted herself to the responsibilities of a household, the husband could pursue all kinds of development and was not strictly bound by the narrow sense of marriage. The woman found happiness and enjoyed respect as the one who nurtured her children, while the husband extended himself outwardly. Being a wife made her head of the household, and her position was not altered by any newly-created relationship. If a new woman or several other women were enjoyed by her husband, she welcomed them as sisters. In ancient marriages, there were no emotional expectations. The wife could enjoy her life and status without interfering with, or playing against, the life of her husband. The center of her life was her children and home. However, I do not think this kind of peace between husband and wife will ever return. A painless marriage must be organized differently today. Otherwise, the unhealthy environment of modern life, or the fear of being married, becomes a problem which causes men and women to lose the root of life and home.

The problem is not one of marriage or of staying together or of making friends. In totality, the problem is one of finding the right partner. Even so, the right partner is always in a process of change.

A good marriage is a balance of love, respect and tolerance. A less than good marriage can sometimes last because of emotional dependency, loneliness, insecurity, or social expectation. If marriage is motivated by the pressures of loneliness, the communication within that marriage will never be complete. This type of marriage is made out of emotional imbalance, and the chance for divorce is already there, but hidden.

Marriage is too high a price to pay in order to drive away loneliness. There are alternatives. Engaging art or participating in spiritual community activities are two positive methods to drive away loneliness and retain emotional balance.

Loneliness can cause people to become imbalanced; it cannot be neglected. All too often loneliness is the source of many bad habits, many bad marriages, many bad occupations and many criminal actions. For a spiritually-developed person, loneliness, or being alone, is a good time for self-cultivation or work. So whether one is alone, in a marriage, or within a group, life must continue to be viewed as a process of cultivation.

During the time the *I Ching* was written, at least 3,000 years ago, highly developed Taoist men and women came together on high energy days to harmonize their energies. Following the old traditional methods conducted by the elders, they practiced the subtle harmonization of yin and yang. In the villages of those ancient times, boys and girls lived separately. The girls usually lived with their families and the boys usually lived in groups. Sexual activity occurred only when a certain age and level of physical maturity had been reached.

For a mind longing for sexual satisfaction, subtle energy integration and cultivation is the best solution. It is the best cure for sexual craving which ordinary playboy-style sex will never achieve. The latter brings about venereal disease, monetary and energy expense, and the loss of one's true personality. Unfortunately, the subtle method is only available those who are spiritually developed.

On several occasions and places in this sacred book, I have revealed that the Integral Way is not the rigid practice of religion which insists upon celibacy. Nor is it the secular way which promotes sexual indulgence. In the Integral Way, one can perform the energy harmonization that remedies the imbalance of natural physical desires without resorting to masturbation or going to any special place. Furthermore, energy harmonization can occur respectfully with, or sometimes without, the knowledge or agreement of a partner. When one is harmonized within, he or she is ready to be re-charged with the different kind of sexual energy the universe provides.

If mental love exists between two people, and if they are virgins and are correctly guided, they can directly become subtly integrated and rank as angels. If they are not virgins, then the couple has more work to do in the subtle integration. If they use their relationship for ordinary sexual intercourse rather than for conceiving a child, it becomes the downfall of their spiritual cultivation.

To suppress love in one's mind or regard the opposite sex or sexual activity as sinful is the narrow practice of religion and is both inhuman and immoral. From this perspective, I appreciate the great value of the different levels of yin and yang harmonization in the Integral Way. The correct practice in this aspect can be learned from my work. One can refer to *Eight Thousand Years of Wisdom, Harmony: The Art of Life* and my other books for guidelines for correct sexual practice.

It is not that marriage is bad; rather, it is people who create problems. They cannot control themselves and harmonize their personal, individual energy.

In the small community of a family, and between husband and wife, brothers and sisters, or parents and children, if one does not maintain a consistent level of one's personality, then the hurt which results is unavoidable. One does not need to study people around the world to see that they poison each other. One merely needs to experience life with those under the same roof to discover that the poison there is stronger than in other places. Total spiritual development in a family is important in order to avoid such poison, but if just one member of the family or group does not develop himself, then his or her behavior becomes a source of unhappiness for the entire family. However, spiritual development cannot be demanded of anyone. The best way of living is to live independently and enjoy a life with no disturbances, especially for one who aspires spiritually. To know one's own range of health or how far one needs to keep oneself from people depends upon one's personal development and needs.

For a spiritually developed person, the Old Master has set this example: "Keep a healthy distance away from people and live with a sufficient amount of private space, even within a family. Yet work selflessly among them."

Note: Spiritually-aware people may think the way of subtle intercourse is the same as tantra, but this is not so. Tantric sex requires penetration or a "plug-in." Subtle intercourse does not require a "plug-in;" it is a communication somewhat like a wireless telephone. It can be practiced anywhere, even with great distances between the two partners, and is far more effective than tantra.

There are three levels of techniques available to our modern times for yin/yang harmonization:

1) For fun. There is no need for this tradition to be taught here since several books on Taoist sex have been translated and are available in book stores.

2) To maintain energy and rejuvenation. At this level, one can not only enjoy sexual activity, but can at the same time pacify the restless mind and enjoy high achievement, rejuvenation and longevity.

3) To approach immortality. This level is the highest means of cultivation.

One of the ways which served as the highest, most secret and most effective method of rejuvenation and longevity was through a dual cultivation which was only practiced in ancient China. This high method no longer exists in our drastically changed world.

Among all the available practices for maintaining and improving health and preparing for visible and invisible sexual cultivation, one may be trained in two typical methods that can be practiced before and after sexual cultivation.

1) The Taoist Way of Vitalization through the Breathing Method: a unique method to strengthen personal vitality and to improve one's physical power and sexual endurance.

2) The Taoist Way of Endurance of Life through Energy Guidance: a special way of working on the glands and the internal flow of energy. It is applied by using a series of quiet sitting movements with the purpose of enforcing one's vitality to slow down the aging process and prevent weakness.

Chapter 55

The Tai Chi of Events

Be gentle in doing right.
Do not be violent.
Be diligent in all undertakings, even in small matters.
The essence of work is diligence.
A successful life depends on doing the right thing
  at the right time and obeying the cosmic law.
Blessings come in many ways.
Do not look for happiness
  and contentment will come naturally.

Continuously remove the negativity within yourself.
One's good life is decided by one's virtue
  and clean mind.
To endure difficulty, avoid complaining.
To endure vexation and annoyance,
  avoid bitter comments.
If your mind is always occupied by distress,
  good fortune is sure to evade you.
When things reach their worst,
  they can only get better.
When something reaches its limit,
  it turns into its opposite.
This is the Tai Chi of events.

Avoid involvement with people who are suspicious,
  easily pleased or angered.
Listen only to viewpoints that are balanced.
Walk away from idle talk.
Unite with people of outstanding character.
Collective purposes form fortresses.
In uniting harmonized energies, we gather strength.

Chapter 56

Cultivate the Tao

Life is a journey.
What is your destination?
Which path will you follow?
The Natural Integral Way differs
  from all ordinary religions and teachings.
We think all people are born
  with the same basic qualities:
  organic, rational and divine in nature.
Right cultivation nourishes these qualities
  enabling fulfillment and union with true life.
Instead of dividing ourselves many times,
  we must nurse the powerful chi.
Books alone will not uncover it.
At birth a person is full of pure chi.
In the process of growing,
  the original one chi divides itself to be three
  as the origin of the productive force,
  the working force, and the mind.
In one's natural healthy life,
the word "virtue" is used as the direction of life.
The three forces will achieve
  the three purities respectively.
To achieve the three purities
  means the fulfillment of the three natures of life.
To develop and fulfill your organic nature
  is to extend to the Realm of Great Purity.
To develop and fulfill your rational nature
  is to extend to the realm of Crystal Purity.
To develop and fulfill your spiritual nature
  is to extend to the Realm of Utmost Purity.
Thus, the realms of life extend to the realms of purity.
The fulfillment of this energy
  is the way of Heaven and Earth.
It has no beginning or end.
It is unchanged and never exhausted.

If not distorted or disturbed,
   it brings proof of immortality.
Because of your place in life,
   there is need for discipline and cultivation.
But this need not be done in the mountains
   as a hermit.
Work with all the changes and patterns
   that life presents you.
Utilize the sacred methods
   to attract the help you need.
Practice it constantly to practice it correctly.
Talk brings no real benefit.
Do not swim in theory, going round and round.
To deepen in reality, cultivate the Tao.

Chapter 57

Spiritual Renaissance

Soen, the name of hexagram 57 ䷸ , means to follow. What do we follow? On what occasion should we be obedient? Let us ponder this spiritual matter.

As a child, I often had the opportunity to see folk people walk barefoot over burning coals at religious festivals. Several times I even saw people with bare feet climb high ladders made of sharp knives. When I was older, I saw someone put a wide knife blade to his chest with his left hand and, with his right hand, use a rolling pin to hit it completely into his chest. Throughout this amazing feat, the performer continually summoned spirits. When the knife was removed, not only was there no bloodshed, there was not even a scratch.

Over the years, I experienced many such extraordinary religious and magical powers. Sometimes I enjoyed them and felt quite amused, but since these feats of magic were not my real interest, I never thought to learn or practice them. Most were without true spiritual development and simply demonstrated "brutal" human faith. Faith that is not guided by reason is brutal; it is a remnant of primitive, undeveloped human tribalism.

Once a divine being said to me, "Humankind's growth is slow. It seems that it has not evolved beyond the 'brutal' stage. For example, modern religions still follow the track of earlier, undeveloped human tribes. They continue to exalt a forceful image of past religious leaders to lord it over present-day people who lack true spiritual knowledge. A certain over-used book is infused into the minds of ordinary people and far-fetched interpretations of this book are produced to fit all situations, while the 'living book' of individual self-cultivation for personal growth is suppressed.

"History is a good book; it demonstrates that old tracks of a failing vehicle should not be followed. When a book containing experiences of brutal struggles of the past is used as the model for present and coming generations, is it not intended to use mixed-up religious emotions to lock people into the same tragic patterns as past generations?

"Hundreds of different interpretations have been given for this book, but they merely compete for authority on something which fundamentally is not a matter of truth or untruth, but rather one of faith. When faith, which is an emotional force itself, is used to guide all other emotional forces, the result is disaster. The stronger an emotional force, the further it is from the truth.

"Surely, throughout the history of humankind we have witnessed many misunderstandings and failures due to lack of spiritual development. They are so obvious that it is not necessary to be spiritually advanced to recognize them. Even the initial leaders of Communism knew them well and utilized these old techniques to push their "new" religion onto people. The form was altered, but the same darkness was imparted. Of course, one would not wish for the world to remain constantly unchanged, but one can wish the quality of human existence to continue to improve. Until the darkness of the human world is totally dispersed by humankind itself, people will never be able to see the light.

"The first Renaissance brought about a change in forms. Let us hope that a new Renaissance will bring about a change in the 'brutal force' which is cultivated by modern civilization.

"Modern people take a meticulous approach to studying the material sphere, but they are lax in studying the reality of the spiritual realm. If the same vigor that is applied toward studying the material sphere could be applied toward studying spiritual reality, dominating, undeveloped religions would cease to control those who are spiritually undeveloped. Most human disputes, based as they are in ignorance and misdirected energy, could then be stopped."

The new Renaissance of humankind is not impossible, but, as most of you know, the strength of the collective good-will of humankind has been misguided and misused. If each of us were to correct this in ourselves, who would say that a new Renaissance of balanced human nature and the above conversation were merely the illusion of a man of cultivation?

Chapter 58

Follow the Plain Truth of Nature

One can be amused by beautiful words.
One also tries to frequently please others
    by what he says.
Are we aware of what we say?
Much speech is not good.
Less speech is favorable.
Speechlessness is best.
Unite your energy to the mystery of the universe,
    and in the quiet depth within yourself
    you will meet the totality of universal truth.

Keep the three mystics (mouth, mind and will)
    firmly united in one.
Roaming, thinking and myth-creating are wasteful.
Hold fast to the true origin of life.
This is of real value to cultivation.
To follow many religious teachings is confusing.
To follow their essence is useful.
To follow some plain truth of nature is best.
Too many methods bewilder.
Use only one path to the most subtle realms.

The deepest mysteries are found
    without any teachings.
Only by being of the highest spirit
    can you be among the Shiens, the whole beings.

Chapter 59

From Three to Five

Dispersion occurs when human intelligence grows above spiritual capability, and when one or a society is unable to be held as one piece. Intellectual divergence arises from the different capabilities that people have for understanding and knowing things. Arguments and wars breed in the warm bed of divergence.

Real peace cannot be achieved until the entire knowing capability is achieved by both the individual and the total human race. Tolerance must be worked at when dealing with such differences. The real strength for such tolerance is only obtained through a higher vision.

Many years ago, a new group of religious leaders from a large city wished to begin a united religious movement. They sought my father's support and expressed their broad-minded views to him in this way:

"All religions are the same. Some people call the universal divinity God, others call it Allah, Brahman, Tao or some other name. The lotus flower sits above its root and its stem and is known by different names in different places, but the lotus at the top and is actually the essence of them all. Therefore, God, Allah, Brahman, Tao and the various other names really mean the top, the essence. Religious conflict is totally unnecessary. Religious teachings should serve people, not cause them to fight over their differences in belief.

"A new universal religion with an equal view and no prejudice is needed now to break through the religious obstacles which have continually hindered a close and peaceful relationship among people throughout the world."

My father greeted them warmly and, during the abundant meal he shared with them, he spoke of his personal efforts in this direction. "I lost my father between the late Spring and early Summer when I was eight years old. At that time, our village and ten neighboring villages were suffering severely from an epidemic of smallpox. It happened that my father was the only doctor people would trust with their young ones' lives, so for three to four months he refused no house call when there was a child with a high fever. Without concern for his own health, without proper rest or food, he fought this vicious, life-taking disease with a firm will day and night and succeeded. Not a single life was lost. Finally, when the difficult period had been overcome, he returned home one evening from a house call. The starlit sky was hushed in silence as he approached the stone bridge crossing the canal. He lifted his over-worked legs, step by weary step, until he finally reached the bridge. In the dark of midnight, the arched bridge of slippery green stones made it difficult for him to cross the canal. The silence surrounded him and everything was peaceful, except for the one thunderous splash from the water. His neatly-cut slim silhouette disappeared from the top of the bridge. At that moment, ten villages and our neighborhood lost a good doctor and I lost my father and teacher of Tao.

"When I was fourteen, I became an apprentice to a tailor who specialized in making religious robes and clothing for priests and monks and nuns of different orders. During this time I had the opportunity to live in one temple after another working for a master of some religion or another. When I was nineteen, I took all my earnings plus my family savings of several hundred pieces of silver and became a military officer. I inherited my rank from one of my uncles who had served in the army of the Ching Dynasty (1644-1911 A.D.)

"My unit was stationed on a beautiful mountain with several famous temples and many hermits who cultivated themselves in the stone caves. The army was sent there because of outlaws who often made this sacred place their den. To pass the time, the soldiers would shoot at monkeys, but since it was such a task to operate the old-fashioned rifles, the monkeys usually disappeared before the soldier could fire a shot. Nevertheless, a rifle in hand always suggested authority, and in my innocent youth I vaguely sought to have some feeling of authority over life and death.

"As I patrolled the different places of the mountain, I became familiar with almost every spiritual person living there. One day, at a place called the Temple of the Benevolent One, I met a traveler. He was a beautiful old man with a lovely moustache and beard and a strong aura around his peaceful being. After a normal greeting I immediately recognized him as a highly achieved one, and a special friendship was formed. Feeling at ease, I asked him about Tao. His straightforward answer surprised me: 'To be an authority of life is to learn the Tao.'

"I laughed and said, 'I am already an authority of life. If I wish, I can kill almost anything on this mountain.'

"'Perhaps you can,' he replied, 'but, it seems to me that killing is not the authority of life. When the chi of death extends itself to someone's hand to execute its work, one becomes the slave of death. An authority of life is the opposite: one who can control his own life can bring life to all others.'

"I paused momentarily to reflect on the wise words this old man had spoken and then continued. 'As a matter of fact, my father was a doctor. He brought life to many families, but lost his own. Thus, a family of long lineage in Tao has been interrupted by his death, and now I have no way to continue his work or career.'

"'See, you are not an authority of life. A person who is an authority of life can determine and achieve what he is going to be. No matter how difficult, all obstacles on his path can be overcome if he applies his utmost sincerity. Tell me if I am not right.'

"After a long, inspiring conversation, I knew I wanted to become his pupil and to follow him wherever he might go, but when I expressed my desire to become his follower he refused, saying, 'I am like an unanchored boat. I am not suitable to have a pupil. But I will make you this promise, every few years I will come to see you.'

"'How will you know where I am?'

"'Do not worry, I shall meet you anywhere, just as I have picked you from among the many soldiers here.'

"I parted from him reluctantly, and since I had also finished my three hundred days of killing authority, I was free to embark on my re-awakened spiritual journey.

"With my skill in making clothes, I visited many spiritual people living in temples, and even some hermits. I stayed here and there for different periods of time in order to learn herbology, acupuncture and Taoism from the many spiritual teachers I encountered along the way. Whenever I heard of anyone who had made some special achievement in his cultivation, I would go there and insist on becoming his pupil. During this time I also finished reading all the books my father had left.

"Ten years passed, and all my teachers thought I was fully skilled and completely knowledgeable in handling all diseases and spiritual problems. With my old, worn robe, oil-paper umbrella, and three pieces of silver, I went to a town to begin my work. This was thirty-five years ago when I was in my thirties. Every day I treated patients, and every festival day I taught people. Soon I found it necessary to develop centers and temples for my teachings, as many people came to accept and practice them. At the opening of one new center I gave the following talk:

"'Give up the prejudices of different religions and use the essence of them all. Recognize the different functions of all teachings. What one can do, another cannot. What Confucius offers is on the level of the general relationship of family and society. What Sakyamuni offers is the consolation of psychological emptiness and the end of death. What Lao Tzu offers is the value of remaining pure and unattached. We need them all. There is no reason for an ardent follower of one religion to be the cruel enemy of another.

"'We are not poor cooks, however, who merely throw a variety of foods together in one dish. We have the highest example from the *I Ching*: the principle of balance. A normal mind is a balanced mind. We should not allow prejudice or the extreme nature of some religions to obstruct our minds and cause difficulty in the practical sphere of life or in the harmonious relationship of mankind. With this principle, I shall call our path the Path of Three-in-One. But it is not limited to three-in-one. The teachings of all great world religions can be melted into one great pot to nourish us. However, I shall still call our group Observers of the Path of Three-in-One. Heaven is one, Earth is one and all religions which are a human development, are one. In a fundamental sense, the body, mind and spirit are reintegrated. Not only do we harmonize with all beings and all world religions, we also unite with all Heavens and Earths in the entire universe.'

"While I was joyfully expressing this new spiritual direction for humanity, I was surprised to see my old friend, the achieved one, among the listeners. He was carrying the same big bamboo hat on his back and was smiling calmly as he sat on one of the seats and quietly listened to my talk. As I went over to greet him, ready to invite him to our home, I was surprised to notice that he appeared exactly as he had the day I last saw him many years ago. When I reached him, he said he wished to see me in the garden to have a word with me.

"After accompanying me to the garden he said: 'What you say is on the conceptual level. The mind is describable; the spirit is not. Tao, as a path, began before recorded history. Thus, there are some things which cannot be described or written about in books. You say that you have gotten the essence of Taoism, but according to all Taoist sages what can be spoken is actually the dregs and is not the essence. You can feed an ordinary horse with general fodder, but you cannot feed a dragon with the food of ordinary people. If this is what you have fed yourself, how do you expect to continue the work of the dragons, your Taoist forefathers? Have you really learned Taoism? Work on this. I will see you in the future.'

"I knew I could not keep him for more instruction. I stood there motionlessly in the garden as he left, while the large crowd somewhere in the distance was enjoying what I had just fed them.

"Beginning at that moment I rearranged my schedule. Almost every afternoon I went to a particular mountain and stayed in seclusion. I meditated on top of a large stone which had a legendary connection with an ancient achieved one. I knew that in order to learn the high truth of life, no ordinary teacher or book could help me. My teacher had to be the old man, my old friend. I thought of him day and night when my mind was clear, and especially when I meditated in seclusion. By doing nothing for several years in my meditation except to think of the old man, I discovered that my mental capability had improved considerably.

One afternoon, during the good weather of autumn, as I was recovering from deep meditation, I discovered an erect, unusual human form in front of me. It was no one else but my old friend!

"He smiled and asked, 'Why do you invite me here?'

"I knew this was the opportunity I had obtained through the practice of utmost sincerity over these long years. I corrected my posture and knelt in front of him. 'Other than to learn Tao from you, I have nothing to beg,' was my prompt reply.

"He laughed and said: 'Tao is too big to put into words. One can only learn a way to reach Tao.'

"'That is what I meant.'

"'From ancient times there have been many methods which were left to be passed on. Some of those methods are used to affect people's vision, such as making oneself disappear, making the sun or moon move eastward, cutting the rainbow in half, spilling beans and transforming them into an army, moving a mountain from one place to another, emptying water from the ocean and so forth. Some ways can cause the full response of nature, such as summoning the wind and rain or thunder to subdue an evil demon or summoning an army of spiritual beings in an important event, or causing flesh to grow again on a skeleton. Some are personal, practical achievements such as traveling to the sun, the moon, and all other stars; making oneself invisible, standing in the sun without casting a shadow; taking a single step and yet traveling thousands of miles; enjoying whatever one wishes that is unobtainable by ordinary people; entering the smallest space, and so forth. Now, what do you wish to learn with such sublimeness?'

"'I wish I could meet my father.' I could not help but ignore all those other interesting methods and directly state what was deepest in my heart. To be with my father again was the only serious wish in my life, although I was soon to discover it would take a long period of cultivation in order to be fulfilled.

"He laughed again. 'You are wishing to make this proof your achievement. But, as you told me, you lost your father when you were a small child.'

"'As I learned, there are five ways of exuviation for one who has achieved himself spiritually. He could have passed through any one of the five ways to dissolve his physical body: spontaneous dissolution (instant departure from any position one chooses and at any time), water dissolution (to be drowned in water), fire dissolution (to be burned in fire), weapon dissolution (to let another person use a weapon on him), and earth dissolution (to make the earth split, bury oneself, and then close it again without a trace). I am certain my father did not die an ordinary death. He must have passed through water dissolution.'

"'How did you know all this? How could you know it was water dissolution?'

"'I read one of my father's secret books and also recall his special virtuous practice. He had clearly made his preparation to enter the Divine Immortal Realm.'

"'In what way would you like to meet your father? As he was in the ordinary world, so that you might see him honorably revered as a human noble? Or would you like to see him as a real divine being?'

"'I would like to see him as a real divine one.'

"'Do you know there are only two important sentences which can describe a divine being? The biggest has no exterior. The smallest has no interior. A divine being is a being who can have the greatest size, or any size or form he chooses for his transformation. Just as a human stretches and bends his body, a divine being stretches, becoming larger than the universe, and bends, becoming smaller than a grain of sand.'

"'I would like to see him as the largest body,' I replied.

"'If he appears as the largest body, you will never recognize him. For example, once when you were on this mountain you felt lost, until suddenly you came to this particular place. Everything was so attractive and precious to you, so beautiful and wonderful. Do you recall how you felt when everything was bathed in abundant sunshine? You were totally enveloped by the charm of this natural environment. Were you not puzzled that you did not know where you were or know how to find this place again afterward? But you did experience it, and you could remember everything in detail, right? Actually, that was your father's divine being; you came into his being. You were active in his being, but you never recognized your father. This is why the divine being can be defined as 'the biggest has no exterior.'

"'Yes, it has always puzzled me. Thank you for breaking the riddle. It is no wonder that there are many legends about people going to places as enchanted as a fairyland, yet not being able to find it again. Now I understand this experience of entering a divine being. It is like a rose placed in a room with its fragrance pervading the entire room. One enters into the being of the rose when one sits in the room, enveloped by its fragrance. Now, please, I would like to see my father in the smallest size.'

"'You could not see him that way either. For example, when you see things, he can be riding on your eyebrow; when you hear things, he can be sitting in your ear. He can be with you any time and any place he wishes, but you cannot see him. It is not his fault that you cannot see him; rather, it is your fault that you have not yet achieved yourself. Your father has been with you many times. There are also hundreds and thousands of divine beings who have visited you, but you have never been able to see them.'

"'Is there a way in which I can meet my father as I see you, the way I talk to you and touch you, as a solid fact which my unevolved human mental pattern can recognized?'

"'You can have the ability from the ancient divine methods to be whatever you wish, as well as to be the size you wish. Your method will be ready for you in your inner room. When you are achieved, I shall bring you to meet your father. Goodbye until next time.'

"He disappeared in the blink of an eye. I hurried home to my inner room. The divine book was on the desk. From that moment on, I gave up conceptual activity and completely engaged myself in real, useful cultivation.

"Another fourteen years passed as I diligently cultivated myself. One late summer afternoon, I was at one of our connected temples, resting by the side of a pond. I was surrounded by weeping willow trees with their long, pliant branches dancing gracefully in the gentle breeze. I watched the lotus flowers in full bloom. In this great tranquility, I saw a familiar figure appear on the surface of the lucid water. Immediately, I turned and stood up to greet my old friend.

" He said, 'I have made an arrangement with your father. He wishes to meet you. We think you are ready!

"'When? And where?' I asked excitedly.

"'Right now. And here. Make arrangements to have no disturbances for seven days.'

"I followed his instructions and made the arrangements. Under his further instructions we meditated there at the side of the pond. The tall cupola of one lotus was the destination we were to reach and enter.

"After I entered the cupola it was no longer a cupola, but a complete universe. I walked with my old friend and occasionally we talked cheerfully. It took us three days to reach the center where, on the central mountain, a figure was sitting gracefully and comfortably. I hastened my steps until I reached where he sat. With every part of my being, I recognized him. He looked the same as he had when I was eight years old, when he had patted my head and then left to make his last house visit. I almost burst into tears with great rapture on finding my father. Finally, after all my valuable toils, I met him.

"My father took my hand and said, 'Let us travel together to see the world. I arrived not long ago.'

"It seemed that all the things I wanted to say to him became like ice exposed to sunshine; they all suddenly disappeared and the three of us happily traveled the interesting world of the cupola.

"Almost seven days had passed when my father said, 'Your body is still important. You have seen me as you wished, and we have had a wonderful time together. This is not a departure, but a new communication to start hereafter. The secret of life and the secret of the universe are ordinary to us, but these secrets are beyond the general human mind. No disturbance should be given to ordinary people or to yourself by telling your experience. This is a traditional prohibition.'

"I bowed to my father, as a human father, who accepted my great human traditional salutation. Then my old friend and I flew back to the shore. After this experience, I revised my view of life and of the world."

Being a student and pupil of my father, I was captivated by this wondrous story as it was being told. I was a bit amazed and uncertain, however, when a small distinct voice arose and said, "Oh, oh, your father made a mistake; he used the food worthy of a dragon to nourish the common people!"

The voice said this with such loud laughter that my ear itched. I could see my father must have received this message at the same moment, for he concluded his story like this:

"From that time on, I corrected my teachings from the Path of the Three-in-One to the Path of the Five-in-One. Dear friends, the Path of the Five-in-One means that the five elementary forces of nature within oneself need to be harmonized. It also means that the five great harmonious relationships and duties on the human level need to be fulfilled, especially the five blessings of Hsin (the divine immortal tradition started before written history): longevity, wealth, health and peace, constant observance of virtue, and natural life. This was the real religion of unspoiled minds, but how can unspoiled minds have such great demands? They did not obtain these five blessings in the relative sphere. They obtained them by birth and by living correctly every moment in life. If we could restore the unspoiled happy mind, what then would we have to unite?"

Chapter 60

"To Do is to Be" and "To Know is To Do"

Discipline and self-restraint are the means of reaching achievement. In fact, they are "achievement" in themselves. In order to avoid an unnatural and immoral result of discipline and self-restraint, the relationship between the discipline and the disciplined must be clearly understood.

Any given action is a reaction to previous behavior, and all behavior and actions are part of all other actions, thus their interaction composes all of life's activities. When we are hungry, we eat. In this case hunger is the cause and eating the effect. We eat in order to satisfy our hunger. Then, when we eat in order to satisfy our hunger, eating becomes the cause and the satisfaction or extinction of hunger becomes the effect. The matter of eating and the satisfaction of hunger are actually of one origin and not two as it may appear.

The one origin is the life force. The entire universe is but a life force called primal energy or universal Nature. Every phenomenon, including non-existence, is a diversified expression of this universal life force or Nature which is self-regulated toward all events in life, big or small.

In the *I Ching* or *The Book of Changes*, this life force of the universe is called Chyan ☰. The expression of the sixty-four hexagrams makes this self-regulated universal law able to be traced.

On a human level, the only constant factor upon which we can rely throughout all generations is the virtue of universal cyclic change. Among all changes and variations, the basic pattern of change has been found in the interaction of yin and yang from which the oneness of primal energy can be recognized.

The relative nature of human cognition is surpassed by spiritual power. An absolute being is one who has extended his knowing and being beyond the relative spheres of general conceptual life. Such spirit of absoluteness is obtained through the experience of relative patterns of the function of mind and finally goes beyond such a relative mind to reach unity.

According to this vision, the highest power in the responsive universe is the power of virtue. The power of virtue maintains the constancy of the universe. Without this constancy, the universe would be in a state of chaos. All of our activities, good or bad, follow a specific, corresponding pattern or channel of energy. Regardless of circumstances, we need to keep our virtue constant. Whether we are rich or poor, noble or common, whether we are having a good day or a bad day, we must always have the same good virtue towards ourselves and others. We need to follow the example of Nature, whose constant virtue enables all beings to have the potential of enjoying their life within their own period of time and development.

As human beings, we are all born with the potential to develop our understanding and our ability to know that the constant virtue of the universe exists behind the changeable, superficial phenomena. Our confidence in Nature first grew from the constant virtue of the universe. All of the world's cultures, religions and sages spoke to their different communities and times in an attempt to describe the truth of life, but their colorful descriptions were variable and never sufficient. Behind all changing phenomena is the hidden, enduring virtue of the universe which, as the universal cycles evolve, remains eternally positive, creative, constructive, productive and affirmative. Because the universe maintains its constant virtue, it never dies. Creatures die because they allow their external environment to continually change their nature and virtue. People are tempted by the outside world and do not feel content and sufficient within their own being. Thus, when they see this, they want to be like this. When they see that, they want to be like that. They forsake their own good nature in the pursuit of something or someone else. They die, not from the moment they physically cease to breathe, but rather in each moment that they lose their constant virtue.

Then what is Tao? Tao is the eternal Way. Tao is the constancy of the universe itself. It is our original, divine, vital energy. With it, we receive life. Without it, we cease to live. Maintaining the enduring spirit of life is the first principle of Taoism. As we remain undisturbed by the changeable face of life, our happiness will never cease and our positive energy will never die but will exist firmly with the eternal Tao.

In ordinary daily life, our primary endeavor is to keep our enduring, positive attributes, whether we are having a good or a bad day. We accept any external change as it is. Relatively speaking, if we keep our virtue, we can enjoy our good days more fully and we can soften and mitigate the discomfort of our bad days. Through virtuous behavior we can even alter possible dangerous situations because of the trustful, stable, true power of constant virtue.

To be virtuous means that we follow the constant Middle Way, not allowing ourselves to run into extremity, violence or radical attitudes. One does not wish to become a Buddha or an angel or any other exalted being. Neither does one want to become evil under any circumstances. We would rather keep our original virtue. We keep our spirit pure and untouched, our mind clear and detached, and especially avoid emotional demands such as emotional prayer and love. We keep our body still and upright (but keeping still does not mean sitting in a corner or lying in the fetal position).

All action must hold a deep respect for the original, productive quietness, the creative nothingness, the most integral, active non-action. Through integral active non-action we can extend the clarity of the mind and innocence of the pristine spirit to embrace the eternal Tao. We spontaneously maintain all our simple, daily activities within the energy track of our life and follow the universal principle of normalcy. This is the way of perpetual peace, beauty, true enjoyment, happiness and spiritual joyousness. This is the secret of a Taoist life.

In Tao, to know is to do and to do is to be. If our knowledge or our spirituality and morality cannot be manifested in our daily lives through our thoughts, attitudes and behavior, it means that we do not truly know them. To know means to have mentally and spiritually attained and experienced it. For example, true knowledge of benevolence is at the same time the manifestation of benevolence in our nature. To know benevolence is to be benevolent.

For instance, a baby may crawl into a busy street because of the negligence of its young mother, and a passer-by may reach out to save the baby from danger. To know is to do. This natural logic expresses the truth that there is no separation between the knower and that which is known or between the doer and that which is done. This truth disproves the erroneous idea that there is separation and duality between what one is and what one thinks, knows, does or experiences on any level. Through such incomplete understanding, mankind dogmatically created such concepts as karma, retribution and the law of cause and effect.

In order to correct the old misinterpretation of natural truth, and to reveal the unchangeable fact that we are what we do and think, this ancient book of the unspoiled mind (the *I Ching*) is presented as an expression of the spiritual truth of behavior. It is, at the same time, a manifestation of the truly wise and virtuous energy of the ancient sages. When a fragrant flower emits its beautiful scent, this is an act complete in itself. The conduct of the follower manifests the nature of a fragrant flower. It does what it is. Otherwise, it would be impossible to recognize it as a fragrant flower. In the absolute realm of spiritual truth, to do is to be. To know is to do. In reality, this is absolute truth.

The act of knowing is the activity of mental energy which forms itself into a specific pattern. The principle "to know is to do" means that the mind extends itself in the projection of mental energy, creating patterns and images which are spontaneously reflected or mirrored back to the mind. In the relative realm, the form or patterns the mind holds may be classified as "good" or "bad." The principle "to know is to do" is different in the relative realm, as one may know something and not necessarily do or be that which one knows.

Comparatively speaking, to truly know something is different from being aware of it. In the realm of mankind, one may discern something as good and thus do good, and one may discern something as bad, but not necessarily do it. This is the basis upon which mankind's codes of ethics and reflections on morality were built. The spiritual, absolute realm transcends duality. In this realm, the mind plays a passive rather than active role - its function is that of a highly sensitive transmitter and receiver which spontaneously knows things without the necessity of previous experience and without having to discriminate between being or doing good or bad.

Chapter 61

Reality

Looking carefully into the truth of spirituality from its origin, one finds that it can only be expressed by the sign ☷ . In this hexagram, two broken lines are between four solid lines, which represents a pure, open and empty mind. In the last five thousand years of cultural development, numerous beliefs, customs and doctrines have been created and established that have either promoted or deterred the spiritual growth of mankind. The fact that differences exist need not be the "problem" that it often is in today's society. Instead, humanity needs to develop the understanding that these differences are only varying recognitions and expressions of different levels of spiritual achievement.

Spiritually developed people are greatly amused and entertained by these colorful differences. They can enjoy the variation without becoming attached or confused. Being on the level of high truth, they do not need to accept or reject anything that was created by people of different times and geographical backgrounds, but such confusion has been the cause of many wars and conflict among undeveloped people.

Collecting the truth of religious reality, as it pertains to the evolution of the rational mind, is valuable. In this way, spiritual confusion can be eliminated and true spiritual essence can be reached. Let us follow the inquisitive mind of an excellent businessman and learn from his experiences in the search for truth.

In a large Chinese city lived a successful businessman. When he was in his teens, he was a Confucian scholar, as were most young men of general education. He came from a poor family, and when his parents died he was forced to give up his studies and become part of the business world. Through hard work and fortunate circumstances he made a substantial fortune by the time he reached his forties. In his personal life, he enjoyed nice houses, beautiful gardens and the comforts of a family. He satisfied himself and his family with the best foods, even delicacies he had never dreamed of in his childhood.

His beloved parents remained deep in his memory, however, and it troubled him that they could not share and enjoy his prosperity. One of his old friends suggested to him a conventional solution.

"It is an easy matter and will only cost you the equivalent of 'one hair from nine cattle' to send your parents to Heaven. Why don't you invite all the different religious groups to perform their rituals to guarantee your parents' ascension to Heaven? This is the way to fulfill your filial duty to your deceased parents."

"But which way works?" the rich man asked.

"Who knows? This is our conventional way. You can see for yourself that this is the custom of all Chinese people when their parents die. They send for Taoist priests, Buddhist monks and nuns, and others to perform different rituals that will allow the dead to ascend to Heaven. One of these methods will probably work, but who knows which, since each one claims to be 'the way.'"

The rich man decided to follow his friend's advice. With some help, he was able to choose the best groups for this special occasion and great rituals were performed for forty-nine days. As people flocked to see them, his feelings changed from sadness to pride. Although he experienced and observed many rituals and ceremonies concerning death, after the busy days had ended he again expressed concern to his friend by asking, "Did any method work?"

"This is the conventional way, as I previously told you. No one seriously questions it. People pay for these rituals in order to feel that they have helped their deceased ones. This is the only answer I know."

The businessman said, "Surely, you and I are successful businessmen. In the business world we have learned to be realistic. I do not mind the money being spent, but I do wonder which way works. I would like to do more for my parents."

"This is not like buying goods for such a good price that you should buy more!" said his friend.

Reluctantly, the rich businessman gave up the idea of doing more, but year after year the many religious questions about death grew deeper in his mind. But as he began to approach fifty, some of his old friends passed away, and he noticed that his body was not as strong as before, so he began contemplating things he had never before taken seriously.

He had many experiences that had helped him solve many problems and difficulties in both his business and daily life, but now he needed a new idea. If money could send people to Heaven, he would surely have no problem, but going to Heaven only occurs after death and no one could prove that it really happens. Taking it for granted was certainly a great risk! He did not mind spending money on rituals if they were effective, but if they were not, then his good soul could be ruined. This might be a serious mistake, especially since his wealth would not be well used. He also thought that if money could buy permission to enter Heaven, all the evil people who had grand rituals performed or who made donations to temples would also go to Heaven. How could a place like "Heaven" be so undiscriminating?

After careful thought, he reached the logical conclusion that money could offer no assurance of going to Heaven. Finally, there came the light from his good business mind that although money could not buy Heaven, it could buy the truth of "reality." Thus, he decided to interview different knowledgeable religious people, and other experienced ones, in order to obtain this "truth" from their learning and experience. He would pay them, of course, as in any other business transaction.

As a good businessman, the adventurousness of this enterprise appealed to him. Though he did not mind paying the price, the goods must be real and worthwhile. If he could gather the correct information to prepare himself for going to a different world, then the money would surely be well spent. At least he would be the only one to blame, regardless of the result.

His idea was not difficult to carry out; only special arrangements needed to be made. A list of good teachers who could present their traditions and practices was prepared. Through the help of experienced friends, the businessman wished to filter out similar theories and practices of the different religions in order to extract the essential truth of each. He was so anxious to know the reality of all these different teachings that he was willing to pay a great sum, with "essence" being his only demand. Since he did not have much time for a great deal of theory, and in order to avoid complication, only the most important teachings were given. His good mind, which had been used so well in the business world, was now being applied as a meticulous buyer in the religious market.

Years passed and he became knowledgeable about all the great religions, including their histories, doctrines and rituals. He remained self-motivated by his untiring inquisitiveness. During the process of learning, he sometimes became subject to the prejudices, confusion and contradictions of particular religions until he was able to attain some degree of enlightenment. Due to this benefit, he could deeply reflect and clearly understand that all dogmatic religious subjectivity, confusion and contradiction are merely conceptual. In other words, they are merely many different creations of the mind.

Surely, this was not what he had originally hoped for. He wished to achieve something deeper and broader than just the general understanding of religions. He now knew that general teachers could not meet his needs. They could only teach him some small things, most of which were theological exaggerations designed to accommodate psychological weaknesses. The structures of those religions did not go beyond the emotional or conceptual level, thus they amounted to no more than toys, tranquilizers, substitutes, compensation and escape. Surely, this shallowness was far from spiritual reality, so he decided to find a teacher who was really achieved, one of the ultimate truth, to be his model.

Finding such a teacher was difficult. Only after searching for many years and using many sources was one of true achievement finally found who would accept the businessman as his student. Before this teacher arrived, the rich man received guidance from his advisor on how to greet a Taoist master. In the teacher's presence he should only present a request or a question and avoid initiating conversation or asking personal questions such as the teacher's age. These questions would find no answers. The rich businessman learned this etiquette and promised to follow it carefully. When the meeting occurred, he welcomed his teacher respectfully, but forgot how to conduct the conversation without asking his teacher's age. The teacher smiled and after a long pause, said:

"The ageless past is my yesterday. The endless future is my tomorrow. From this immeasurable present, at the point of this instant, you and I are meeting. The Realm of Timelessness is where I live, where neither time nor age are measured. Using no measurement, we can accept people as they really are."

The businessman suddenly recalled the warning he had received from his advisor. He immediately begged forgiveness and straightforwardly presented his wish to learn Tao.

The teacher demanded twelve fish of pure gold, each weighing one catty (16 Chinese ounces of gold) to be placed in a boat along with other offerings. The boat would set sail and be secluded from the worldly life of people. Only deaf sailors and servants would be allowed to help in the boat.

After everything was prepared, and on an auspicious day, the teacher and pupil sailed out to sea accompanied by a few sailors and servants. The servants helped prepare the offerings in the manner of traditional ritual and then retreated behind their partition at the rear of the cabin. Only the teacher and the pupil were left together. They ceremoniously made offerings to the Heavenly Realm. Then, to the amazement of the rich businessman, the teacher took the gold fish and threw them one by one into the ocean. The pupil's first instinct was to stop him, but he dared not since the fish no longer belonged to him.

Finally, he gathered his courage and asked the master, "May I venture to ask the meaning of this?"

The teacher's answer was simple: "I just wanted to see the fish swim again."

"I am afraid that probably cannot happen."

"Why not?"

"Lifeless gold cannot be made into living fish."

"Is it that your gold is not good enough?"

"All gold is lifeless, venerable sir."

The teacher then smiled and gently said to his pupil "I am glad you also know that."

At first the rich pupil was stricken, realizing what an expensive lesson he had just been taught, but he immediately said to his teacher, "Thank you sir. Hereafter, your pupil will not value all those lifeless things. I will maintain single-mindedness in order to learn Tao from you."

"Being a truthful one, what do you already know about the achievement of Tao?"

"I know thus far in order to learn Tao, self-cultivation is more valued than common worship. The purpose of self-cultivation is to achieve natural self-mastery, self-discipline, self-dependence, self-continence, self-improvement, self-restraint, self-communion, self-command, self-possession, self-realization, self-sufficiency, self-contentment, self-effacement, self-renunciation and self-surrender. However, among all of these words, none can be considered an exact meaning for Taoist cultivation; they are only a measure."

"What makes self-cultivation different from other paths?"

"In all popular religions, authority exists outside of, not within, one's life. Therefore, worship is considered to be the most important practice of all general religions. In Taoism, however, one begins with a foundation of sincere practice and the recognition that the authority of life is within one's own being. One thus achieves the realization of true inner authority. Therefore, the process of self-cultivation is the main feature of Taoism.

"I do not mean that because Taoism stresses self-cultivation, one needs to turn away from the Divine Realm. I mean that only through one's own self-cultivation can one attain spiritual growth. Through this process of growth, one can connect deeply with the Divine Realm.

"In the real practice of Taoism, one realizes the divinity within oneself; there is no real separation between the universal nature and one's own divine nature. In the practice of popular religion, a divine authority is established outside of one's own being. As the followers of these religions miss the spiritual truth of oneness and become

dualistic, the Divine Realm becomes even further removed
from their lives. In practicing self-cultivation, however, one
should not put too much emphasis on one's personal,
individual divinity in order not to lose connection with the
total divinity.

"There is nothing wrong with the level you have
reached," continued the teacher, "what else do you wish to
learn?"

"Not the conceptual level, but how to truly achieve Tao,"
the man answered.

"In order to achieve Tao and become divine within and
without, one has to complete one's virtue. Only by realizing
and cultivating one's virtue can the secret of achieving Tao
be passed on to a person," the teacher replied.

"Your pupil will do whatever you suggest," said the
businessman.

"Did you ever lose your virtue as you made those lifeless
fish?"

The businessman collected his thoughts and prudently
made the following statement, "No sir. I assume you are
asking if I lost my virtue in my financial enterprises. I have
truly known that I dare not sever my root of life from its
Heavenly source, and have made a continuous effort to keep
myself on the right path. Within this busily changing world,
I am a man of diligence, sincerity, honesty, earnestness,
duty, prudence, carefulness, fortitude, bravery, temperance,
order, decency, courage and cleanliness. Among my friends
and acquaintances I have earned a reputation as a man of
righteousness, faithfulness, loyalty, trustworthiness, justice,
helpfulness, kindness, gentleness, harmony, cooperation,
courtesy, politeness, consideration, understanding, forgiveness and charity. In my own work of business management, I am a man of fidelity, propriety, correctness, exact-
ness, precision and efficiency. I am also scrupulous in
making money and frugal in spending it. For this, my
family has occasionally complained. However, I believe I am
frugal, not miserly. Every evening before going to bed, I
write in my diary as a means of introspection. I have
practiced this for many years. While this is my realization
of self-virtue in everyday life, I truly know this is not

something I did for others. I did it for myself, and it is nothing to be proud of. I have not accumulated any merit for the world. I have been self-centered with my love, and my purpose in life has been to obtain worldly strength. I was a man of the world, yet I recognize that divinity and Heaven are manifested by their boundless, virtuous love; that spirits can be made to respond to sincerity; and that the nature of the universe is the fundamental reality of the universe. The virtue of nature is to be truthful. Virtue is long-enduring; any other kind of power or force is short-lived. Virtue is gentle and subtle; power or force is strong and conspicuous. I am vaguely aware that through self-cultivation one can restore the virtue of one's nature regardless of birth, education or social background, but I made virtue the decoration of my life, the hallmark of being well-bred, an exhibition of my high social standing. I was wrong. Since I became interested in Tao, I now know that virtue exists in the honest, plain nature of a human being and can be expressed in various ways. Plain nature is invariable at any given time.

"My virtue was fragmented. I did not have integrity. Although my enlightenment is late, I now know that all virtue can be summarized into one word: goodness. Goodness is the first nature of all beings. When goodness is used to describe the first nature, it is the nature of truth, beauty, sacredness, perfection, completeness and greatness. In reality, the first nature cannot be specified by any particular virtue. Thus, it is truly integrally virtuous.

"Evil and sin caused by experiences within the social environment are distortions of the original, true nature. Self-contamination and bad habits are actually our second or false nature. Usually, someone who remains trapped in this way of living is referred to as one who has lost his original nature. Understanding this, I know that our original nature is invariable nature itself. It is the path, the Way. Consequently, following the path is truly self-realization and self-accomplishment.

"The first nature of human beings is the very nature of Heaven and Earth and, by extension, the nature of the entire universe. All correct spiritual education is aimed at the restoration of this original nature. This restoration does not require one to 'work' on anything. As I was told, the purest guidance of 'non-doing,' 'non-making' or 'non-deviating' is the only proper method. In order to recover our lost nature and reintegrate the many deviations from this nature, one has to eliminate contaminations from one's practical daily life. Such contamination is sometimes called using 'expedient measures' and, in certain situations, may be the most appropriate or the only way to react.

"But persisting in 'expedient measures' can become a means for corrupting one's nature. For example, in ancient Chinese society, bodily touch or extreme closeness between sisters and brothers, fathers and daughters, mothers and sons, brothers-in-law and sisters-in-law was strictly forbidden in order to avoid antagonisms or the possibility of interbreeding. Once the ancient sage, Mencius, was challenged with a question: 'If a sister-in-law fell into a well, should a brother-in-law reach his hand in to save her?" Mencius responded that he should, for this was an example of an expedient condition, not a normal one.

"However, if expedient behavior becomes habit-forming, such as helping one's sister-in-law in everyday situations, then many troubles may arise. In this same manner, soldiers carry out many evil orders during war; however, such expedient actions should not become habitual in one's daily life after times of war.

"Evil and sin can be defined as actions and behavior which occur at improper times and places. They are not absolute. Evil people and real sinners are those who become attached to expedient behavior once they discover this is an easy way of solving problems or accomplishing their purpose. Therefore, these expedient measures become habits, routines, and eventually a way of life. People who cultivate themselves do not need to work in order to reclaim their original nature; instead they need to constantly cleanse and purify the dirt that they touch. One must be careful not to let habits become the master of one's life.

"In cultivating the Integral Way, one cultivates the virtue of self-integration. In meditating on the Integral Way, one awakens the virtue of one's original nature. Awakening and enlightenment are not a form of spiritual loftiness, but come from a thorough realization of virtue.

"Cultivating Tao restores the integrity of the innate, universal, natural being. Cultivation restores purity to mental and physical contamination. Cultivation reintegrates the fragments of worldly distractions and de-unifying experiences. To be integral is to be one with the true, deep nature of the universe.

"Because the nature of human beings is the nature of the universe, the authority of life is internal. The authority of judgment is also internal and parallels the growth of human self-awareness. Punishment and guilt, misery and suffering are the results of deviating from one's original nature. Reward, contentment and true happiness all come from the constancy of embracing one's original nature. The highest morality is not linked to the demands of society, but comes from total inner harmony and balance. Thus, high morality is not a result of preaching; it is a result of self-recognition.

"The Integral Way is indescribable because it is total integration, but among all individually expressed virtues, truthfulness and sincerity are pivotal. With sincerity, one can realize one's true integral being. Virtue is like a beautiful flower, with one's integral nature as the root. The realization of virtue does not come from working frag-mentedly on the surface of one's personality. Virtue must be whole, not partial. This is called 'Integral Being.'

"People all know that being virtuous is a valuable thing, but only a few know that being virtuous can be used as a 'secret measure' or 'weapon' for a nation, a family or a person to improve inner and outer being. Virtue can be practiced in a secret way as a silent path. Otherwise, one might turn virtue into something superficial and thus not be benefitted by one's practices. By taking credit for virtuous actions, the mind is easily disturbed and sometimes even destroyed. Examples of this behavior are apparent in situations of worldly conflict. Therefore, the subtle, secret virtue is highest.

"What I have sincerely done through all the many years of preparation is just for this moment, in order for me to be worthy to receive the treasures of Tao. I present this to you for your inspection, sir."

The master responded, "The virtue I inquire about is much more fundamental than you might think. It is basic to all human life and does not involve philosophical understanding. Please, tell me: Do you eat well? Do you sleep well? Do you eliminate well? Do you do well with women? Do you walk well? These are some of the virtues of a normal, healthy life. If one has trouble with any of these, one may wonder what were the true reasons their life was ruined. I hope you have not neglected these."

"In all honesty, venerable teacher, with regard to these personal things my life is thus: after years of beneficial and unbeneficial pursuits I have a stomach ulcer, so I cannot eat well. In terms of sleep, I have frequent insomnia, so I cannot sleep well. In terms of elimination, I have habitual constipation, so I cannot have good bowel movements. In terms of urination, I have kidney stones, so I cannot eliminate well. In terms of sex, I cannot have an erection, so I feel impotent. In terms of walking long distances, I have gout in both knees, so I cannot walk far. In terms of ..."

The teacher stopped him. "That is enough to tell me that you have lost the virtue of a basic life. What kind of Taoism do you expect to learn from me?"

"To integrally achieve in Tao," was the determined response.

"First," instructed the teacher, "restore all the virtues of a basic life. I do not need to question you further in order to find out whether you are worthy. Only when you restore these basic virtues shall the secret of Tao be passed on to you."

The rich businessman followed the special instructions and method his teacher passed on to him and restored all the "virtues" he had lost. In his later years he enjoyed the health of a total being. On various occasions, many of his old friends would visit him and ask how to cultivate Tao. He always laughed and gave an answer like this:

"As I was taught, the spiritual realm is not very different from doing business in the ordinary world. One needs to be practical about one's personal cultivation. One must first fulfill all aspects of life in order to live a life of completeness. This does not involve enormous material possessions, rather, a life of completeness is in itself the very essence of life. It cannot be achieved without being practical or down to earth.

"I have come to understand that spiritual achievement is purely personal. One's practice must be subtle and secret. In other words, be a god in the Subtle Realm and not a force in the human realm. This is spiritual virtue. One can be a spiritual model for people, while being careful not to present a dominant spiritual image, since this only creates conflict. If one loses spiritual virtue, one's teachings may sound beautiful, but they have no real spiritual value. Do not be confused by the great world religions. Do not mistake scarecrows for real beings. Do not choose a religion which will make you narrow and prejudiced. Always respect real spiritual education which can help you grow. Total human spiritual growth can only be realized through individual spiritual growth. By practicing true piety, which is not misguided toward a narrowly defined, limited spiritual image, one can find a connection with the totality of universal life. By achieving clarity, one can transcend shallow cultural and religious conflict. This clarity also allows one to be indifferent to the troublesome, vulgar world of ignorance, obstinacy and aggression.

"I have learned to cherish the truth in life. I believe the truth within me to be the same truth of other lives. It is not the truth which causes troubles; it is the inflexibility of many different interpretations which causes the major problems in the ordinary human world.

"The main thing I have gained from my search and the self-cultivation which I now enjoy and can share with others is this: depart from the wasteful past. Refine and enhance the essence of your being in order to live a universal life of endless bounty."

The businessman enjoyed great personal benefits as a result of learning Tao and his spiritual growth was much advanced. One day, to his surprise, he was paid a visit by Master True Gold. On this precious occasion, he sought further instruction. After this visit from his teacher, the man further taught his friends.

"After learning Tao, we are proud of our good health. Having good health is nice, but it is not the total meaning of achieving Tao. If so, lions and tigers and other wild animals that have good health would be achieved in Tao. We also enjoy the high view that we have cultivated. But are you aware that you are taking advantage of that which is low to build that which is high? Surely, there should be no pride in this achievement either. Moreover, you inflexibly apply the principle of balance to all situations, which tells me you do not truly understand what balance is.

"Contrary to popular misconception, balance is not something that is half of this and half of that, though it can be equivalent and symmetrical. The correct application of balance is not a "middle" or "halfway," nor an attitude of compromise.

"In ☰ ☰ and ☷ different cycles which are beginning should be handled accordingly.

"In ☲ ☴ and ☵ different centers of strength are formed; one is broad-purposed and the other is narrow-purposed.

"In ☶ ☳ and ☱ responsibility is given; one undertaken with humility, the other with caution.

"In ☴ ☳ and ☵ duties are assigned to assistants. Privileges also shift to them. One accepts some with confidence and others with fear.

"In ☵ ☲ and ☷ correct centers are recognized; one supportive of kindness and the other of egoless power.

"In ☰ ☰ and ☷ competition is expressed; one with aggressive dominance, the other with virtuous resolution.

"In ☷ and ☶ ☴ the energy is different, but in the same formation. Here, the balancing center is the fifth line. When the center lines are all strong, ☰, the second line expresses safety, but in ☶ ☴ the top line sacrifices itself for the rest. In ☳ ☴, not only does the vitality of the masculine energy return, but also that of the feminine in ☴ ☴; and, as the vitality of the masculine energy leaves, so does the feminine.

"In all sixty-four hexagrams there must be a balancing line. The application of this principle is unlimited. For example: the proportion of ocean water to earth surface is 70/30. In this case, it is the necessary and appropriate balance. Similarly, the hemispheres of the earth, like the hemispheres of the brain, are not a 50/50 division. Their true equivalence or balance comes instead from the way in which they interact.

This same general principle applies to everything. In diet and nutrition, for instance, the correct balance is not 50% yang-natured food to 50% yin-natured food, rather it is four portions of yang-natured food to one portion of yin-natured food. (Note: this can be interpreted as a balanced proportion between alkaline and acid foods.)

Also consider the "lopsided" but nonetheless healthy balance within the human body, such as the vast number of red blood cells (i.e., the yung, or nutritive blood) working harmoniously with the small band of white blood cells (the wei, or protective blood). By virtue of their respective functions, it would create havoc if they were equal in number.

"Extending outward into the social sphere, we can observe many instances in which the idea of a 50/50 balance should not and will not work. It would only be a source of misery. For example, when a country attempts to spend half or more of its budget on national defense, resulting in the necessary neglect of all other positive and beneficial causes, such as education, transportation, technological development and social welfare. In this case, true "balance" would be achieved at a level closer to 70/30, with the military being apportioned the lesser share.

"Analogously, ever reflective of Nature, the sixty-four hexagrams express different patterns of energy formation. In each hexagram, one appropriate point must be found. Only when that point is discovered and realized can balance, harmony and good cooperation exist.

"In every situation, there is an area or zone in which a harmonious balance of yin-yang is maintained. If the boundary for this zone is overstepped, one will meet destruction, and the particular transgression will naturally meet its appropriate retribution. Regarding individual life, the trouble will affect the person, his family, and all that he is associated with. On a larger scale, the effect is naturally much bigger. There have been many people in history who have tried to cross the harmonizing boundary line of yin-yang, even to the limitation of extremes at both ends, and have thus met destruction as a result of their personal ambition. In all matters and relationships, this inviolable line of harmony can never be ignored.

"Those of development need to learn how to muffle their voices and not only understand the importance of realizing their virtuous being, but also keep it unknown to others. Never be proud of building something outwardly, but at all times, embody the unborn, imperishable and Immortal One."

Chapter 62

Avoiding Excess in Everyday Life

When practicing self-cultivation,
 be truthful.
Continually assess your achievement.
With the Sacred Method of Harmony,
 dissolve the concept of self.
Prove that beingness and emptiness are connected
 and mutually transforming.

Life and death are superficial phenomena.
The way of life and death is one, not two.
Control the energy,
 and true living continues endlessly.

Because your energy is not yet refined,
 you become disturbed
 during the early stages of cultivation.
Eventually, the essence
 of the abdominal center appears,
 changing to sweet and fragrant chi.
Breaking through the three main points of the spine,
 these energy transformations
 can have the following benefit.
Rising up from the kidneys,
 the energy penetrates directly into the brain,
 becoming spiritual light,
 the energy of life and regeneration.

To achieve and constantly maintain the three spheres,
 agile vitality, calm mind and high pure spirit,
 proves that you are already a shien
 living in this world.
Govern your body with your spirit
 in order to progress to a higher level of life.
You are asked not only to inwardly cultivate
 your spiritual essence,
 but also to live harmoniously in the world.

To live in the world,
    we must complete the three natures of life
    (the divine, the human, and the transcendent)
    and become integrated with
    the virtue of mellowness.
To measure the success of self-cultivation,
    do not use the conceptual gauges of
    failure, success, sharpness or dullness.
Look only for the purity that comes from
    sublimating confused discrepancies.
This comes from uniting with Tao.

A broken ship cannot journey long on the ocean.
In parting from the Truth to cling to false worship,
    deception and exaggeration bring only emptiness.
From an impure, dirt-filled world you can grow
    to become a tall, pure lotus.
Forsake all wasteful wandering,
    all nonsensical talk and theories.
Nourish yourself with the true chi of original oneness.

Chapter 63

The Integral Life

No one can neglect the importance of the material in maintaining life. This is an obvious fact which people may tend to overvalue by taking the view that one's physical life is the entirety of one's true being. The spiritually developed individual knows that the limitation of a lifetime is a limitation of view, and that it falls short of the total reality of life.

In human life, each individual has a subtle essence which can be treated as the core of one's being. This subtle essence is formed prior to the physical form and returns to the subtle sphere after the physical form ceases to exist. This subtle, spiritual essence can be weakened and scattered, or strengthened through life experience.

Most people have not discovered this truth of life, thus they make a cheap trade by misusing the eternal subtle essence to serve the needs of their material life. On the other hand, it is also an error for people of spiritual quality to focus solely on the subtle and neglect the material. They do not fulfill the balanced path of life and thus lose the opportunity of holistic development in life. Worst of all, many people become lost in the confusion of the multiple misconceptions of cultural religious viewpoints which are limited by the background of time and affected with only short term goals.

The following story presents the reflection of a universal mind to another open mind of a high human being.

Several million years ago, astral beings lived on energy islands in space. Some of these islands were close to our solar system, and over a long period of time these beings witnessed the small planet earth becoming a balanced field of different energies that radiated from far and nearby stars and planets.

After some time, this balanced planet became a place on which a new specimen of life could thrive and propagate. The appearance of this new specimen, which was highly intelligent and which had a perfectly shaped physical body, gave all the astral beings such great joy that they came to earth to play with and teach these human beings.

To their astonishment, the astral beings recognized that this new species grew so intelligent that the original balance and well-being of individuals could no longer be maintained. Extreme tendencies became more and more prevalent. As human beings became increasingly superficial, they eventually lost the spiritual essence of their life. This improper development caused the astral friends great concern, and most of them stopped visiting the earth as often as they used to.

One astral family, however, could not bear to see the darkening of the human race. In order to help mankind rediscover its original balance, integrity and clarity, this family decided to take upon itself the task of enlightening their spiritual human friends. Thus it was that some six thousand years ago those kind astral beings came to this world and took human form in order to help humanity overcome its difficulties. They knew that taking human form could hinder their own spiritual clarity, but an effort had to be made.

They decided that the two hundredth cycle of the yellowish planet, Saturn, as it orbits the Sun, would be the time for them to meet again, (One orbit of Saturn around the sun takes approximately 30 years) and that their meeting place could be the top of Kun Lun mountain, the designated station point for space traveling. They also decided that after their meeting they would restore themselves to divine immortality and play no more reincarnating games in the human realm.

For six thousand years, these astral beings had many human lives. They were good swimmers in the stream of life. Just as a swimmer holds his breath and submerges his head into the water, then lifts his head up into the fresh air, the astral beings would complete each life cycle, occasionally leaving the water to take a rest and sit on the shore. With such attained freedom, one does not become attached to either the joy of swimming or the leisure of sitting on the shore. Whatever is done is done with the highest freedom.

Time came for the meeting. Although all the astral beings lived in different places, had different kinds of lives and different appearances, a strong summons was simultaneously felt in each of their hearts. One by one, they all came to Kun Lun mountain in the Western region of China where gatherings of immortal astral beings often take place. They all arrived on time and quietly refreshed themselves. Although they recalled who they had been and the work they had performed on earth, they had completely awakened from their experiences of human life. Their total integrity was restored.

Before returning to the Divine Immortal Realm, however, they each offered what they had witnessed in the human realm. What follows are their conversations, as reflected in the mind of one of their human friends. We should regard it as advice the immortals have offered to us.

Chia, from the East of Kun Lun said: "I have witnessed both the growth and decline of our human friends. They have become trapped by their own creations: social systems, religions and other such weapons. Their common problem is the lack of spiritual clarity. Although they can intelligently handle small matters, they are unable to perceive the whole. They enthusiastically pursue external or material expansion which results only in upsetting their naturally well-balanced lives. Greed leads them away from their innermost spiritual source. Unlike the ancient, integrally developed human beings, modern intellectuals can see tiny things in hidden places, but due to the lack of inner awareness, they are unable to see the vast spiritual truth, even if it was a cart of firewood right in front of their eyes! Being able to see a detail in the material sphere can be useful, but insisting that what one sees is the total truth is a serious mistake that can create unnecessary conflict and disharmony among human societies."

Yi, from the Southeast of Kun Lun, said: "I am concerned that our human friends have misguided their emotions in the direction of darkness. It is not religious emotion or pure piety that creates problems, but war-like religious structures with dominant doctrines, aggressive

temperaments, and racially ignorant prejudice that eventually lead all followers into an abyss.

"Piety, like any other human emotion, can have a positive effect if it is well-balanced and correctly guided. If not,
it can negatively influence both an individual and the entire
human race.

"With their spiritual focus misguided and misused, our
human friends have lost their natural direction and seek the
temporary relief that some religions offer. They cannot see
that the most important element of a religion should not be
fear of some god who is a source of power or force. The
positive basis of all true religion is sincerity, not fear.
Whatever form sincerity or piety takes is strictly superficial.
A religion is only the framework or house for one's piety.
Once this is understood, then one can also understand that
piety within and between all people is the same; the only
difference is in its various expressions and interpretations.
Without sincerity, all religious worship, sacrifice, offerings,
and rituals become meaningless. Thus, competition or
contention among religions is fundamentally groundless."

Bing, from the South of Kun Lun, said: "If our human
friends knew that piety is their own internal, boundless
treasure, and if their piety were correctly guided and conducted, then they would discover the universal truth of all
life.

"No one can be forced to only one way of interpreting
the truth. It is more appropriate to show people true
sincerity. A sincere person is a developed one; discrimination cannot affect one of pure piety and sincerity. Although
stories can describe piety, they are only stories. Religious
conflicts exist because people insist that their interpretation
is the only conceivable one. Although ordinary religion
serves as a means of interpretation, the higher truth is
indescribable personal sincerity.

"People and societies that are oppressed tend to respond
to religions with rigidly narrow social views. Also, without
a negative environment, people might not engage in individual spiritual growth. However, they do not need to settle for
the kind of worship where only a single element of piety is

expressed, but should inwardly recognize their divine nature.

"External religions worship the shell of spiritual custom such as what God looks like, what kind of robe God wears, what kind of crown is on God's head, what God holds in his hand, etc. But the True Path values reaching the purity that is beyond description or interpretation and achieving subtle integration with the high spiritual reality of the universal nature. Awe is merely a preliminary passion or an emotion to support religion as the establishment of an external image of authority. True piety and a pure mind, however, enable one to remain inwardly centered and to achieve the highest spiritual level: a serene mind and the stability of pure spiritual energy.

"Divine beings respond differently in different situations. They respond in ways that communicate certain messages, or in ways that are only understandable to a particular person. The appearance of a divine being is a message or a communication in itself. However, a defined form or single interpretation cannot be ascribed to a divine being. In most situations, if a person is developed enough, he will be the only person who receives and understands the message. To become dogmatic is thus harmful.

"The highest Divine Realm, as achieved by the most ancient developed people, is correctly expressed as the 'Three Purities:' The Form of the Formless, The Image of the Imageless, The Shape of the Shapeless. This means that the divine form is not limited, the divine image is not a single image, and the divine shape is not one definite shape. The Divine Realm reflects an image that does not have to wear white, purple, or any other specific color or garment. Nothing can be defined in the real Divine Realm. Thus, the true highest Divine Realm, the true origin, is the mother of all images, all forms and all shapes.

"Recent converts, or people who are born into a particular religion, are usually not objective about their religion. They are touched by stories which only temporarily correspond in some manner to their emotions and life experiences. As strong sympathizers and firm believers, they reinforce the same patterns of emotion and follow the same pattern of destiny as the religion they follow. This is not a natural, healthy attitude derived from spiritual growth and deep individual awareness.

"The general purpose of established religion is to teach people to worship a single spiritual image for the purpose of authority and power rather than to guide them to achieve true spiritual growth. Individual development is curbed by dogma, which causes people to eventually stray from a liberal-minded, meditative and reflective spiritual path.

"Unfortunately, piety is often only accepted when it is practiced according to a particular, established way. However, this kind of practice becomes the source of religious confusion and conflict in the world. Thus, a complete spiritual education must have two elements which are of equal value for individual development: the practice of pure piety guided by personally developed awareness, and self-cultivation for harmonized development."

Ding, from the Southwest of Kun Lun, said: "The spiritual confusion of the human world is indeed expressed in its religions. Religions have misused the emotion of sincerity or piety; thus, followers never have the opportunity to correctly reach the exquisite reality of spiritual truth. When one's sincerity is aimed at a target such as God or salvation, one must be developed enough to know whether that direction is the correct way. Although most religions use the emotion of sincerity, it is usually misguided. Even with piety, one needs the right direction. However, one does not need to travel far. One's own true essence is the gateway to the high spiritual realm. A pure human mind is like a mirror, and describable images are its reflections. What one projects into the mirror is the image it will reflect.

"Many people have misused the good name of religious faith as a tool for expressing their mischievous qualities and narrow-mindedness. Making a public declaration and spectacle of one's own piety does not necessarily indicate real spiritual growth. Such people have been known to criticize, attack and burn those of different beliefs in order to demonstrate the strength of their piety, but in reality they are totally lost.

"Piety must be rightfully expressed. With true, pure piety, a person will never be wild. With pure piety, one will always be gentle. With true piety, one will never do evil. With pure piety, one will always cherish and maintain purity and clarity."

Geng, from the West of Kun Lun, said: "The false beliefs of our human friends have definitely led them in the wrong direction. The Divine Realm exists above the human realm, but the dominance of a narrowly-defined spiritual realm of strong emotional force is not a true expression of the Divine Realm.

"The Divine Origin, which is expressed as the Subtle Realm, is indescribable, but a society or individual can always be open to various religious interpretations. All interpretations stray from the indefinable Subtle Truth, but such differences can offer further growth, even though they represent only a certain level of mental development. A natural, truthful and sincere mind is above all interpretations and is the totality of spiritual truth.

"A social design, which was given the term 'religion' by earlier leaders, cannot be good for all times and all people. Any religious or political system which imposes rigid patterns on a society must inevitably lead to suffering, pressure and tension. Any benefit, including military 'strength,' is ultimately nullified by the resulting deadlock of inflexible conditions. Compare this to a society that is naturally free and has less armed strength; the people stay open-minded, free, natural and harmonious.

"Those who extend their minds directly to the reality of the spiritual realm and who are not perplexed by the outer forms of religion should be respected. They can live within a rigid worldly structure without losing their clarity of mind. Even while amassing material wealth they can value the spiritual truth without becoming lost.

"Most religions do not intend to guide people in the direction of total spiritual growth. They practice religious enslavement instead of true awakening or enlightenment. Only a developed person can embrace the universe.

"When one embraces the universe, all divine beings are harmonized and connected with him. One does not need to pray in order to obtain their response. It all depends upon whether one uses one's mind broadly or narrowly. Spiritual connectedness is just a measure of what one can achieve.

"The integral path can open the eyes of its followers to see the true purpose of spiritual development. It can also pass on to them methods for their spiritual self-cultivation which will allow them to reach true spiritual reality. Engaging in such practices is indeed personal and real, and is the way to reach the true Divine Origin."

Hsin, from the Northwest of Kun Lun, said: "There is some dispute among modern minds as to how the world began. Those who hold the view of idealism believe the world started as the creation of God. Those who hold the view of materialism believe the world is based on matter. However, long ago some ancient achieved human beings reached the level of discovery that the origin or potency of the universe is chi. The first stage of pure existence is neither mind nor matter, but chi. Mind and matter are merely different expressions of this primal chi. Existence is not a matter of different 'origins,' but of development. Thus, existence can be developed as mind and matter.

"Mental energy is a more highly developed stage of chi derived from grosser, material energy. It is the essence of the external material shell. However, essence cannot be without its gross base.

"The origin of energy has no form. It is pure chi, which is the original form of everything. Thus, the origin of the universe cannot be defined as being either material or mental, it is simply chi. Disputes between materialists and idealists, therefore, have no basis, but are merely the expressions of a limited point of view. Insistence on such partial views becomes the source of disintegration for human society.

"Standards for evaluating success and achievement in the world today may stress material progress, but if material progress goes against human nature, then imbalance occurs and a crisis will develop. In any age, the principle of balance should be the highest guideline. It should also be applied to general religious practices. Religious life has many different levels: social, personal, emotional and spiritual. Fundamentally, if one is to avoid the downfall of human nature, one must become aware enough to rise above all established doctrines which damage the original naturalness and oneness of human nature. Only the unspoiled, natural followers of the ancient integral path can maintain the direct embodiment and fulfillment of truth in their lives.

"If one seeks individual realization of everlasting spiritual life, the methods still exist. The path of total integration is not only valuable for spiritual, mental and physical health and development, but it can also prepare one for high achievement. Actualization of such achievement has been proven by our ancient human friends who achieved themselves through these truthful methods."

Ren, from the North of Kun Lun, said: "In very ancient times, divine immortals could communicate with the unspoiled minds of their human friends. All beings, including humans, are born of Heaven. No group of people is especially favored by God, nor are there individuals who are God-forsaken. Heaven favors those who are virtuous, regardless of their tribe or religion.

"Through virtue and spiritual development, spiritual ascension can be attained. However, it can never be achieved by emotionally worshipping and begging God to do what one wants because one is unable to accomplish it for oneself. Unfortunately, due to the present confusion of people, they cannot follow the education that their immortal friends gave them.

"In ancient times, the divine immortals taught their human friends that universal harmony is the basic virtue of life. Obedience and harmony were originally expressed toward the wholeness called Heaven. This faith was handed down before recorded history, and it recognized two very important elements: the omnipresence of the subtle Heavenly law (Tien Li), and the unimpeded individual conscience, which is able to know the existence of the Heavenly law without searching for it. These were the sole moral strengths of the ancient developed ones before the invention of religion. To unspoiled people, Heavenly law is the mind, and the mind is the Heavenly law that true knowledge is born within.

"Artificial religions, on the other hand, make people behave decently out of fear of being punished by Heaven. This fear is widely preached by all religious leaders and is the degradation of human spiritual dignity. Thus, people are losing the true knowledge of their deep inner root of universal life. Fortunately, the healthy ancient faith has been preserved in three different sources: Lao Tzu, Confucius and Mo Tzu. Lao Tzu interpreted the faith of Heaven as keeping to the original nature. Confucius' philosophy of humanism was based on the fact that Heavenly law is not beyond human nature. And Mo Tzu put it into the solemn practice of universal love.

"Ancient developed people recognized Heaven as their subtle supporter. Interpretations of Heaven as a dominion that is different from what the ancients knew came from later religions. Heaven (Tien) is the universal subtle law residing above all ruling forces. Mo Tzu elucidated it thus: 'Heaven desires righteousness and detests unrighteousness. If I lead people under Heaven to live a life of righteousness, I do as Heaven desires; then Heaven will respond to me with what I desire. What I desire are blessings and benefit. What I detest are calamities and harm. If I lead the people under Heaven to live a life of troublemaking and evil doings, then I do not as Heaven desires, but as Heaven detests. How do I know what Heaven desires and detests? By the fact that under Heaven the one who is righteous lives a natural life, and the one who is unrighteous usually dies unnaturally. One who is righteous enjoys life, one who is unrighteous suffers. One who is righteous receives peace, and one who is unrighteous suffers being disordered. Heaven desires that people live happily and not die unnaturally. Heaven desires people to be self-sufficient and joyful and not suffer from self-created poverty and difficulties. Heaven desires that people live peacefully and not struggle in disorder and confusion. This is how I know that

Heaven desires what is righteous and detests what is unrighteous.'

"This was the invisible law engraved in the minds of these developed people. Can one separate Heavenly nature from human nature? The social code of ancient developed people depended upon self-recognized natural moral law and, as a result, there was mutual understanding and consideration among all people. Even though there were leaders in an ancient system of government, society was naturally ordered without being specifically organized. Modern people may think the old natural societies were backward, yet they were more normal in a healthier, human way. Modern people may think they were random and unorganized, yet they were natural and organic. Modern people may think they were inefficient, yet they were relaxed. Modern people may think they were unsystematized, yet they were flexible.

"The ancient faith of humanism did not function as a regimented system of law or religion which rigidly forced its demands on people. The foundation of ancient society did not depend on emperors or officials for the establishment of order; it depended on an invisible moral force in every individual which was further established within the family. Family discipline was the real foundation of social discipline. Parents took responsibility for the behavior of their children, and the elders took responsibility for the young.

"For almost 5,000 years moral law was the foundation of that society. Until the present time, though the dynasties have changed, the social code did not. The faith in the Subtle Law of Heaven and humanism was the real ruling power of the unspoiled mind. The ancient emperors were not the real rulers; on the contrary, they were the ones who enjoyed the good nature of their people. The real leader on the spiritual throne of China was universal humanism. The society developed naturally, stage by stage.

"However, the seeds of confusion in thinking sprouted like weeds, and the Old Sage, Lao Tzu, saw correctly that the decline of human nature would be inevitable. He beckoned people to return to their original nature, for when one returns to the true mind of simplicity, there is neither confusion nor contention.

"Surely, human life is now much more highly developed than animal life, so why don't humans have peace? Although wild animals are not more highly evolved than humans, they have no organized wars. Competition and war have made all divine beings sad to see the backward direction of human nature. If the human race continues to follow the darkness of its impulsive blindness, it may lead itself to the point of self-extinction.

"The natural faith of humanism, or universal love, is the mellow fruit of and for all people. The ancient developed people directly recognized and applied the principle that Heavenly law is the human mind, and the human mind is Heavenly law. They maintain naturalness without deviation from the truth. A developed person should keep to the balanced, broad perspective without becoming religiously dogmatic. Humanism, or universal love, can be one's contribution to total human life. This is the essence of the individual in human society and it should be the goal of the entire human race."

Gwei, from the Northeast of Kun Lun, said: "The important achievement of the ancient developed people is their holistic comprehension of the universe. This wholeness is the basic expression of the primal chi as numerous small Tai Chi's with indistinguishable qualities, whether mind or matter. The symbol of Tai chi is ☯. Chi is the foremost foundation of the universe before it develops into the distinguishable sphere. Tai chi is many; Tai chi is one. It can be the smallest and the subtlest entity of the universe before any shape is formed. In totality, Tai Chi is the boundlessness of the universe.

"Through manifestation comes the dimension of mind and matter. Even in the ultimate development of both, whether ideological or materialistic, both are still completely within the scope of Tai Chi. In its pure, original state, mind cannot be separated from matter, nor can matter be separated from mind. Nonetheless, an artificial, intellectual separation was made. It was a dichotomy with no basis, the result of a partial vision of the manifested level. On the subtlest level, chi, or first stage of pure, original existence, cannot be called mind or matter. However, it can develop as matter or as mind. It is not different to begin with; it is only perceived as being different.

"Indeed, the growth of the universe is like the growth of all human life. In its early stages, there was the indistinguishable oneness, akin to babyhood, when neither the mind nor the body considered themselves separate or different from each other.

"In the second stage, spirits became active on the gross material level. Spirits were no more than the subtle essence of the gross, bulky material base.

"In the third stage, different levels of spirits formalized themselves with harmonious energy to become life. To take the form of life is to follow the cycles of life and death. To remain a spiritual being is to keep enforcing one's true essence and thereby to surpass the cycles of life and death.

"In the fourth stage, the appearance of human life was the perfect projection and formation of high spiritual beings.

"In the fifth stage, the partial development of humanity's awareness brought about the divergence of mind and body. The result of this dualistic vision was confusion and conflict.

"In the sixth stage, the original human nature was lost by confused creations and social competition. The downfall of humankind portends dangers which are beyond humanity's own capabilities to handle and control.

"In the seventh stage, in which vast destruction is approaching, self-awareness finally grows individually within people and on a cooperative basis. The value of human preservation becomes recognized, and human beings will again appreciate the truth of immortality.

"This is where the further development of human life after 'death' (the death caused by pursuit of worldly pleasures) is revealed. Possibilities exist in one's lifetimes to cultivate, develop and direct the subtle essence in order to enjoy everlasting spiritual freedom."

Mu, from the Upper Region of the Central Land, close to Kun Lun, said: "In order to give real hope to our human friends, it is necessary for them to focus on cultivating the essential quality of their intrinsic nature. All human external characteristics - what school a person graduated from, what position he holds in society, how much money the person has made or plans to make - is not our concern. There is only one true concern: the quality of a person. It is the quality of a person, the way one cultivates, develops and achieves oneself, that is the true measure of nobility. This is the only way to be ranked among the Divine Immortals.

"Needless to say, if one seeks spiritual maturity, there is nothing above the direct spiritual disciplines of the Integral Path. If one seeks continual life without influencing or accepting the interruption from the transformation of lives, the highest secret of the Integral Path is what one should acquire. This is all the truth we can reveal.

"Many animals have the peculiar habit of taking the indirect route home. They prefer the winding path. However, there is no such detour for a human being to take before reaching his or her own 'home.' Studying all the religions in the world may be fine if a person does not become entrapped by them. However, it is mostly a waste in terms of the spiritual maturation necessary to arrive 'home.' One who leads a life of self-cultivation will have the opportunity for full, spiritual growth; one who dogmatically follows a religion will not.

"One who wishes to restore his divine nature through self-cultivation must first recognize that his nature is the universal divine nature. He must then realize the universal divine nature in his life by extending universal love with the principle of balance. Since his life-being is also a life-being of the universal divine nature, he must give his love equally. Therefore, through the realization of universal divine nature through one's self-cultivation, human nature and divine nature are reunited as one. Thus, any achieved one can recognize himself as being the same as God.

"A child's heart enjoys all kinds of different things. It is never bothered by conceptual differences. People, whether young or old, should meet each other with the heart of a child. This is the most important element of the human spirit and the best interpretation of humanism. The spiritual goal of a human being should be the restoration of a child's heart and a fully and healthily developed mind with high intuition and insight."

Syh, from the Lower Region of Central Land, close to Kun Lun, said: "Nature causes death to purify all lives. People accelerate this 'purification' with misdeeds directed towards themselves and others. The content of their lives is that of following the demands of their blind impulses without experiencing true inner growth. Eventually, they will be weeded out by the wars of competition, unnatural accidents and disease, and will endlessly repeat such cycles.

"People of self-awareness, however, continually purify themselves instead of relying on the cycles of nature to do it for them. They cultivate inner spiritual wisdom which becomes the true growth necessary to awaken them from blind worldly impulses.

"By responding to force with force, the human race has inevitably led itself deeper and deeper into new problems and difficulties. Can our human friends return to their original nature? The entire society cannot return to a rustic, natural life, but individual human friends can maintain their good human nature.

"As Lao Tzu says, 'Reaching the Truth calls not for complicating our minds, but rather for returning to simplicity and enjoying peace.'"

Chapter 64

The Unspoiled Natural Religion

Long, long ago I was in a vast land. The people of this land knew of nothing other than their honest life. They lived by earnest means. They all shared the same understanding: if one does not like what a person does to them, then one does not do that to another.

In this community no generation had ever started a war or made war any part of their livelihood. Their language was simple: all words were one syllable, the most common being "Oh" and "Ah." The former was a peaceful greeting for all occasions and the latter was the first sound in everybody's name. All of the people in this community maintained the same unorganized faith which had not been designed by anyone but had evolved naturally.

This was long ago, when people enjoyed a good, natural life. Many years later, suddenly confronted with outside worldly contention, this simple community struggled to maintain its own natural way. However, as new leaders adopted new philosophies and new ways, the people became lost. It seemed as though there was no one left who could recognize the original faith.

I was taught the original faith by my dear Father, Mother, and ageless Master. It had been handed down by the unspoiled ancient mind to provide help for those who needed it. Today, an unspoiled mind no longer exists because of the confusion brought about by human cultures and religions. My experience is no exception, but my faith, which was derived from unspoiled Nature, keeps my mind whole and in good use.

I make the following simple notes in order to retain the original guidance from the natural Divine Realm in my memory and as a means by which people can dissolve all later human prejudices.

The Natural State of Heaven is Impersonal
The original, unspoiled human mind understood that Heaven is impersonal. However, as it became tainted and

confused, so did its view of Heaven, which became personal and anthropomorphic. A pure human mind is an extension of Heaven. All distorted images of Heaven stem from later mental development that was narrative in nature and that does not reflect the natural source of human life.

The value of faith in an impersonal Heaven lies in its not being named or insisted upon by the human mind. No one can justify a conceptual position by claiming divine right or authority. In contrast, ordinary religions, however, are created out of human concepts and explanations, thus providing opportunities for people to take sides, and engage in all kinds of savageries to defend or spread such doctrines. Any religion that deviates from the impersonal purity of divinity eventually becomes a source of conceptual confusion that will spread contention.

One who cherishes faith in an impersonal Heaven lives a life of unselfish achievement. He does not gather people in his name or teach them to worship him or try to dominate them in any other way. Just as the Heavenly bodies offer their light without asking for anything in return, his devotion and work are offered without expectation of personal recognition or reward. Because he truly knows that Heaven or God has no name but can be referred to by all names, he achieves the "Being of Heaven," the non-partial "Being of Wholeness."

Heaven Has No Name

If we use human conceptions to describe Heaven, surely we limit it and make it partial. One's expression of Heaven is limited by one's knowledge and vocabulary, thus confusion and conflict are often created. The ancient, natural faith in Heaven is impersonal and has no particular name. So it is with all Gods; they cannot be defined by conceptual attempts.

The original human beings also had no name. All natural life is without a name. Why then must God have a name? As soon as God is defined, he ceases to be universal and is no longer the truth. God represents all beings and things of the universe and should have no particular name.

To create a name for God is to separate him from his oneness.

Heaven is Limitless

The natural faith of the unspoiled ancient mind recognized that God has no particular shape or form, but the spoiled human mind has since dressed God in distinctive robes. In order to dress God, there must be a suitable tailor and the best cloth. How ridiculous! Giving height, weight, or other personal attributes to God is ludicrous and untrue.

Human mental development has become one-sided and tainted with conceptions. People no longer respond to the bare truth without an explanation or mental interpretation. In ancient times, people did not need mental interpretations because they had direct correspondence with Divine Beings. There were no conceptions which separated real beings from perceived ones.

Modern people have a chronic need to use their minds to interpret the facts of their life experience. Their lives depend on their minds' interpretive systems to explain the meaning of everything, even their feelings. Truly, they do not live a real life; they live by thinking. Thus, they have destroyed their real nature. Their minds have become very complicated and they live in a distorted, conceptual world instead of the real one. Even the simple fact of love or making love is, throughout its duration, continuously defined and described to the mind. All these words and concepts appear in the mind to separate experience from reality. In the same way, modern artificial faith has lost all sight, through its various interpretations, of the natural truth which the ancient developed ones once recognized and followed. Thus, we must recover the real nature as the ancient developed ones.

Heavenly Love is Impartial

The ancient, unspoiled faith believed that God is impartial love. God does not only love people because they are yellow, as yellow as gold, or because they are white, as white as jade. God loves gold, jade, and all colors, and no color. God is impersonal love. The love of men is partial and limited; the love of God is not. God never limits love to one culture or gives partial love to another. Partial love is created through one's own partial reflection. However, such a reflection also gives one much responsibility: it is to repay Heaven in gratitude for this love, and not to become prejudiced. The secret of inviting God's love is to be natural and virtuous. God loves the natural and virtuous.

God Has No Myth
The existence of Heaven is natural. It did not originate in the narrative mind of later human beings. Mythology is the primitive attempt to explain the phenomena of nature. Surprisingly, the ancient faith in Heaven has no mythology. From ancient writings engraved on the bones of oxen, we know certain rituals and the specific purposes and times that offerings were made, but there was no particular myth that was the authorized story of God and Heaven.

There were, however, many myths that mankind devised for himself. One of these was a myth about the first man, who was called Pang Gu or "Disc Head." According to the myth, the sky and earth were originally like a great egg. Pang Gu worked on this lump of energy with his ax to form the sky, the earth, and so forth, thus becoming the first man and ruler of the universe. This is not a myth about Heaven, but the origin of human beings. It originated much later than the longer period of untraceable, ancient times.

There were no myths until the development of the *I Ching* system which used "lines" to tell how the universe began, how it is now, and what it will be like in the future. But the *I Ching* is not a myth; it is an expression of the direct spiritual experience of the natural growth and development of Nature and mankind. It is a wordless interpretation, and was thus the first direct way of expressing the truth.

Human Nature is Heavenly Nature
Another trait of the ancient natural faith is belief in the oneness of Heavenly nature and human nature. True human nature is Heavenly nature; there is no distinction or separation between them. The concept of Heaven and man

as two separate entities developed in later times. The idea of God as divine and man as vulgar is a divergence from the truth. The duality, separation and multiplicity of later generations formed our human nature in a complicated mold, but originally it was the same as Heavenly nature.

One is Many/Many are One

Another essential aspect of natural faith in a universal divinity is that, "One is many, and many are one." Religious conflicts over the question of many gods or one God, polytheism or monotheism, came about in later generations along with philosophical conflicts about monism or pluralism. But the ancient unspoiled mind was not confused. It knew clearly that the Subtle Origin is one and its manifestations, duplications and multiplications are many. Therefore, one is many and, at the same time, many are one.

When the Divine Realm responds to different people at different times for different purposes, it is multiple. In its unmanifest state, it is one. Therefore, in the unspoiled ancient mind, there was never confusion about one God or many gods as there is today in modern religions. One God is many gods; many gods are one God. If we talk about many gods, we are referring to the different responses of the Subtle Realm to a particular group of people at a particular time. The divine nature of the universe is one, but its responsive function is multiple. To insist on one God, or on many gods, is to take a partial, limited view of the Divine Nature or Oneness.

God is the Model of Virtue

Another aspect of the natural faith in Heaven was the recognition of God as the model of virtue. In later times, God became recognized as a model for domination. The ancient faith was practiced by Fu Shi who interpreted the natural truth with the line system, by Shen Nung, the developer of agriculture, and by other ancient sages who all served mankind. The troubles of the world became their troubles, yet they did not hesitate to resign when their work was done, for they were not attached to their positions. They never thought in terms of capitalizing upon their influence by becoming powerful leaders. The term "Ti" was used as a title for God and the human virtuous leaders. Ti has been incorrectly translated in English as "emperor." In Chinese, however, the character for Ti is the image of the stem from which the fruit or flower is sustained. Thus it is the emperor (Ti) who serves the people (the fruit or flowers). In broader terms, God is the stem from which all human beings obtain the sustenance of life. This was the ancient simple faith.

God Provides His Model in the Human World
The ancient developed people were pure people. Those who served the public were capable and virtuous. They received no salary for accepting this responsibility; they freely offered their talents and capabilities to society. Therefore, people trusted their leaders as the elder sons of Heaven, though everybody was considered to be a son or daughter of Heaven.

In later times, usurpers in Chinese history stole the name "Son of Heaven" and used it to rule people. Therefore, no single person, group, or class should be entrusted with the same responsibility as the ancient leaders. No one can believe that modern dictators are the elder sons of Heaven.

For spiritual reasons, one must be personally responsible for oneself. People can no longer naively have faith in their leaders. Generally, if a good leader is chosen, there is safety; if not, then people find themselves in difficulty. Therefore, we must restore the authority of virtue in our own being and become harmonious with other people.

Natural Faith has No Particular Rituals
Another quality of the ancient natural faith is freedom of worship. Confucius gathered and organized all the ancient forms of worship and presented them as the only correct form of worship. Although his purpose was to exemplify the ancient way, it unfortunately limited human piety to formal ritual and thus harmed the naturalness and originality of the ancient unspoiled faith.

During ancient times no one forced people to follow an organized form of worship. Their worship was free. The diversity of their worship grew out of natural differences of expression, however, they were all linked and unified by the same belief in Heaven. There were no problems or conflicts over differences, because a real faith and connection with Heaven existed.

Everything Under Heaven is Equal

Another trait of the ancient unspoiled faith of Heaven was the absence of distinctive social classes. Some societies of later generations have had a strong faith in Heaven, however, they have also created strong class distinctions among people. Class distinction is not the ultimate truth. God loves everybody. There are no special classes worthy of special favors.

God does favor the virtuous, however. The practice of virtue does not belong to any class. Certainly there are natural distinctions among people. Some are wise and some are less developed, and some have great potential while others will never attain greatness even if the opportunity is offered, but these are merely differences, not classes. Such differences are natural. They represent the essence a person develops throughout one or many lifetimes. Surely, there is a difference between a phoenix and a crow, but differences are not the basis on which we can establish respect or disrespect, preference or dislike. In the natural unspoiled faith, no such distinction exists. Social classes are an artificial human establishment and thus a violation of nature. They go against the Heavenly Way.

A Correct Way of Life is the Natural Religion

In the ancient natural faith, religion was nothing other than the correct way of life. There was no need to establish anything else, for the correct way of life was good faith. In later times, people established a religion apart from their lives because the correct way of life had been lost.

When there is a common respect for life, everybody can reach an agreement, but when religions are established on the basis of differences, conflicts arise. Such religion is untruthful because it is unnatural.

Natural Life is the Blessing of Heaven
The ancients recognized that worldly blessings are the rewards of Heaven. To be healthy, to eat and sleep well, to have a balanced mind and live naturally is to be blessed by Heaven. To receive life is the blessing of Heaven. To live peacefully is a blessing in itself. Whatever happens in a normal life is already a blessing. One does not need to look elsewhere for happiness. This only leads to imaginary happiness.

Natural Religion did not Start
with the Preaching of a Particular Book
There was no book from which to preach the ancient unspoiled faith of Heaven. This faith was practiced by seeking divine guidance through a responsive system of change. Important events were engraved on ox bones which have continuously been discovered in underground excavations.

The Book of History was compiled by Confucius from ancient documents which described communities, wars, significant worship of Heaven, ceremonies, celebrations, and more. They also revealed the ancients' simple faith in Heaven. We know that the virtuous leaders of ancient society were recognized as the eldest sons of Heaven. Public decisions, however, were not made by these leaders, but were left to errorless, divine guidance.

During those times there were no distinctions. People knew that the source of all life was nature. Out of respect, they called this nature Heaven or "Ti" (God). To distinguish where they lived, they called it Earth. Earth was the small Heaven; the entire universe was the big Heaven.

This was the only faith for 5,000 years of written history, until recently when new standards were established. These new standards have brought much confusion.

A Natural Religion Seeks Only Divine Guidance
The natural unspoiled religion always sought Divine guidance through divination. Many ancient tribes throughout the world used some system of divination to help them make decisions in life. This system of inquiry expresses

high wisdom since it can encompass all knowledge. Its method is as systematic as scientific and as logical as exact mathematics. It is a highly dialectic philosophical system.

What is the benefit of such a system? Though we are modern educated people, we are impulsive most of the time, and this leads us into difficulty. Indeed, all wars are the result of impulsiveness. As we reflect on our actions, in the hope of curtailing our impulsiveness, perhaps it seems unreasonable to exalt an ancient system above modern high technology. One important advantage of divination, however, is that the activity of divination has a calming effect which to some extent tames impulsiveness. This is how ancient people subdued and educated themselves.

In contemplating the actions of human beings, it is not a question of who is better and who is worse. Rather, it is a matter of who is more reasonable and who is more impulsive; this is what makes the difference. The marvelous aspect of ancient societies was that opinions and decisions affecting the public were not determined by individuals or leaders alone, but by the subtle guidance received through divination.

With this understanding, the differences between natural faith and social religious doctrines can more clearly be seen. It is a question of faith in the natural Subtle Law or in human dogma and doctrines. The ancient faith was not dogmatic. On the contrary, it was founded on the principles of appropriateness and balance in response to change. This is the most essential point in the ancient faith in "always seeking correctness."

The ancient developed people, with their natural unspoiled faith, truly understood and believed that the universe became manifest and was arranged through Subtle Law, which is highest above everything. Behind all human activity is Subtle Law. It is the ultimate law of the universe and of human life. Divination makes an aspect of the Subtle Law apparent and provides guidance in understanding and making a decision about a particular event.

On the basis of these principles, one can decide one's behavior and actions with or without divination. Ancient people had a strong faith in the Subtle Law and followed it exactly. They did not go beyond their own "lines" of duty. This faith was neither blind nor impulsive. On the contrary, it was built by experiment and experience. It was only through experience that the correct interpretations and illustrations of the Subtle Law could be found. We need to rebuild our own faith so that we too can live harmoniously and in accordance with the Subtle Law.

Certainly there can be no harm in following the examples of our ancient ancestors. Without a true and natural faith, modern people have become lost. When the ancient ones received guidance from the Divine Realm, they had no fear. They had no consideration of personal benefit or even of life or death. They integrated their lives with the Subtle Realm and received the instruction of the Subtle Law through either divination or their own discoveries of invaluable principles. Thus they lived a whole-hearted life rather than a fragmented one. Since they had a closer connection with nature, they enjoyed many things. Their minds were not like modern minds which are trapped in thinking. Modern people's way of living is not real living. It is only formalized thoughts, imagination, and interpretations of their own system, which is not a true system.

When you consider the wholeness and simplicity of natural religion, you can see that it is modern people who have become superstitious through the fragmentation of a magnitude of dogma in their minds.

Three Elucidations of the Natural Religion

Before any book was written or any religion was developed, a natural faith existed and was practiced. Later, religion developed and was influenced by specific social backgrounds and problems. Religion was the response to a particular human situation; it does not represent a true faith. This is why we value the unspoiled natural religion.

The unspoiled religion has no particular book. All of human history is a book of the testing faith of religions, whether they have succeeded or failed. Generally speaking, we value every life experience that is connected with the internal and external development and evolution of human life. Whatever is true and natural is where God resides. There is no need to doubt this.

Any particular book, no matter how profound, represents only one interpretation of the Heavenly Realm. An accurate account of history can be a religious book if it records all actions, great deeds as well as great mistakes and transgressions. By reflecting on such events, human beings can better understand their troubles, how they spoil themselves, how they destroy themselves, and how they deviate from their true nature. All good books illustrate the natural, Heavenly Way and thus serve in the discovery and rediscovery of the natural, correct way of life.

In China, three correct elucidations of the natural truth were presented, each somewhat differently, by Lao Tzu, Confucius and Mo Tzu. Lao Tzu served to guide people back to their natural root. During his time there was already much divergence and deviation. He taught people to restore themselves through nature, because only nature can provide the correct direction of life. Anything interpreted by the later spoiled mind is misleading.

Confucius valued humanistic love, or "ren." Within the pit of the apricot, peach or plum is "ren," the essence of life. This means that all life is life-centered. Therefore, in order to realize personal life and to enjoy co-existence one must realize humanistic love.

Mo Tzu expressed three main elements with his teaching: following the Heavenly will, universal love, and non-aggression.

In terms of the ancient tradition, all three (Confucius, Lao Tzu and Mo Tzu) serve equally as primary illustrators of God and Heaven. There is also value in the good interpretations of other religions. However, it is necessary to make some adjustments in order to avoid racial and all other artificial prejudices.

By seeking the oneness of spiritual truth, together we assist the transformation of human society and help establish total progress for the entire human race.

About Taoist Master Ni, Hua Ching

Master Ni, Hua-Ching is fully acknowledged and empowered as a true Master of Tao. He is heir to the wisdom transmitted through an unbroken succession of 74 generations of Taoist Masters dating back to 216 B.C. As a young boy, he was educated within his family in the spiritual foundation of Tao. Later, he studied more than 31 years in the high mountains of China, fully achieving all aspects of Taoist science and metaphysics. This study was done in different stages. According to Master Ni, the best way to live, when possible, is to spend part of your time secluded in the mountains and the other part in the city doing work of a different nature. This is better for the nervous system than staying in only one type of environment.

In addition, 38 generations of the Ni family have practiced natural Taoist medicine. Master Ni has continued this in America with clinics and the establishment of Yo San University of Traditional Chinese Medicine.

Throughout his life, Master Ni has supported himself as a physician. His Taoist teaching over the last 40 years has been as a service to people. He began teaching in Taiwan and after 27 years, came to the United States in 1976. Since then, he has taught throughout the world and has published 18 books in English, produced five videotapes of Taoist movements, and has written several dozen Taoist songs performed by an American singer.

Master Ni has also written 50 books in Chinese including two books about Chinese medicine,five books on Taoist spiritual cultivation and four books about the Chinese internal school of martial arts. These were published in Taiwan.

Thirty-three books were written by brush in Chinese calligraphy during the years in which he attained a certain degree of achievement in his personal spiritual cultivation. Master Ni said, "Those books were written when my spiritual energy was rising to my head to answer the deep questions in my mind. In spiritual self-cultivation, only by nurturing your own internal spirit can communication exist between the internal and external gods. This can be proven by your personal spiritual stature. For example, after nurturing your internal spirit, through your thoughts, you contact many subjects which you could not reach in ordinary daily life. Such spiritual inspiration comes to help when you need it. Writings done with good concentration are almost like meditation and are one fruit of your cultivation. This type of writing is how internal and external spiritual communication can be realized. For the purpose of self-instruction, writing is one important practice of the Jing Ming School or the School of Pure Light. It was beneficial to me as I grew spiritually. I began to write these books when I was a teenager and my spiritual self awareness had begun to grow."

In his books published in Taiwan, Master Ni did not give the details of his spiritual background. It was ancient Taoist custom that all writers, such as Lao Tzu and Chuang Tzu, avoided giving a description of their personal lives. Lao Tzu and Chuang Tzu were not even their given names. However, Master Ni conforms with the modern system of biographies and copyrights to meet the needs of the new society.

Master Ni's teaching differs from what is generally called Taoism in modern times. There is no comparison or relationship between his teaching and conventional folk Taoism. Master Ni describes his independent teaching as having broken away from the narrow concept of lineage or religious mixture of folk Taoism. It is non-conventional and differs from the teaching of other teachers.

Master Ni shares his own achievement as the teaching of rejuvenated Taoism, which has its origins in the prehistoric stages of human life. Master Ni's teaching is the Integral Way or Integral Taoism. It is based on the Three Scriptures of Taoist Mysticism: Lao Tzu's *Tao Teh Ching*, *The Teachings of Chuang Tzu* and *The I Ching (The Book of Changes)*. Master Ni has translated these three classics into versions which accurately carry the most valuable ancient message. His other books provide the material for different stages of learning Tao. With his achieved insight, he has absorbed all the truthful and high spiritual achievements from various schools to assist in the illustration of Tao on different levels of teaching.

The ancient Taoist writing contained in the Three Scriptures of Taoist Mysticism and the Taoist books of many schools were very difficult to understand, even for Chinese scholars. Thus, the real Taoist teaching is not known to scholars of later generations, the Chinese people, or foreign translators. It would have become lost to the world if Master Ni, with his spiritual achievement, had not rewritten it into simple language. In a practical manner, he has revived the ancient teaching to make it useful for all people.

Throughout the world, Master Ni teaches the simple, pure message of his spiritual ancestors to assist modern people in under-standing life and awakening to Tao. Taoist Master Ni, Hua-Ching has spoken out and clearly offered more teaching than any other true Taoist master in history. With his achieved insight, over 80 years of training and teaching, and his deep spiritual commitment, Master Ni shares his own achievement as the pure rejuvenated teaching of the Integral Tao.

BOOKS IN ENGLISH BY MASTER NI

Life and Teaching of Two Immortals, Volume 1: Kou Hong - *New Publication!*
Master Kou Hong was an achieved Taoist Master born into an ordinary family around 283 A.D. in China. He was the first master of Tao to write a responsible book with details about immortal practice. He was also a healer in Traditional Chinese Medicine and a specialist in the art of refining medicines, including immortal medicine. Master Kou Hong successfully refined his golden immortal medicine and ascended during the daytime in 363 A.D. In this book, Master Ni gives important details of Master Kou Hong's life and teaching which are of special interest to those engaged in spiritual cultivation and seeking spiritual benefit of life. 176 pages, softcover, Stock No. BKOUH

Ageless Counsel for Modern Life - *New Publication!*
Master Ni's work entitled *The Book of Changes and the Unchanging Truth,* contains sixty-four illustrative commentaries. Readers have found them meaningful and useful; they cover a variety of topics and give spiritual guidance for everyday life. Many readers requested the commentaries be printed apart from the big text, so we have put them all together in this one volume. The good directions and principles explained here can guide and enrich your life. Master Ni's delightful poetry and some teachings of esoteric Taoism can be found here as well. 256 pages, softcover, Stock No. BAGUI, $15.95.

The Mystical Universal Mother - *New Publication!*
An understanding of both kinds of energies existing in the universe - masculine and feminine - are crucial to the understanding of oneself, in particular for people moving to higher spiritual evolution. In this book, Master Ni focuses upon the feminine as the Mystical Universal Mother and gives examples through the lives of some ancient and modern women, including a woman Taoist teacher known as Mother Chern or the Mother of Yellow Altar, some famous historical Chinese women, the first human woman called Neu Wu, and Master Ni's own mother. 240 pages, softcover, Stock No. bmyst, $14.95

Moonlight in the Dark Night - New Publication!
In order to attain inner clarity and freedom of the soul, you have to get your emotions under control. It seems that spiritual achievement itself is not a great obstacle, once you understand what is helpful and what is not. What is left for most people is their own emotions, which affect the way they treat themselves and others. This will cause trouble for themselves or for other people. This book contains Taoist wisdom on the balancing of the emotions, including balancing love relationships, so that spiritual achievement can become possible. 168 pages, softcover, Stock No. BBECO, $12.95

Harmony - The Art of Life - *New Publication!*
Harmony occurs when two different things find the point at which they can link together. The point of linkage, if healthy and helpful, brings harmony. Harmony is a spiritual matter which relates to each individual's personal sensitivity and sensitivity to each situation of daily life. Basically, harmony comes from understanding yourself. In this book, Master Ni shares some valuable Taoist understanding and insight about the ability to bring harmony within one's own self, one's relationships and the world. 208 pages, Stock No. BHARM, softcover, $14.95

Attune Your Body With Dao-In: Taoist Exercise for a Long and Happy Life - *New Publication!* - Dao-In is a series of typical Taoist movements which are traditionally used for physical energy conducting. These exercises were passed down from the ancient achieved Taoists and immortals. The ancients discovered that Dao-In exercises not only solved problems of stagnant energy, but also increased their health and lengthened their years. The exercises are also used as practical support for cultivation and the higher achievements of spiritual immortality. 144 pages, BDAOI Softcover with photographs, $14.95

The Key to Good Fortune: Refining Your Spirit - *New Publication!* A translation of Straighten Your Way (Tai Shan Kan Yin Pien) and The Silent Way of Blessing (Yin Chia Wen), which are the main guidance for a mature and healthy life. This amplified version of the popular booklet called The Heavenly Way includes a new commentary section by Master Ni which discusses how spiritual improvement can be an integral part of one's life and how to realize a Heavenly life on earth. 144 pages. Stock No. BKEYT. Softcover, $12.95

Eternal Light - *New Publication!*
In this book, Master Ni presents the life and teachings of his father, Grandmaster Ni, Yo San, who was a spiritually achieved person, a Taoist healer and teacher, and a source of inspiration to Master Ni in his life. Here is an intimate look at the lifestyle of a spiritual family. Some of the deeper teachings and understandings of spirituality passed from father to son are clearly given and elucidated. This book is recommended for those committed to living a spiritual way of life and wishing for higher achievement. 208 pages Stock No. BETER Softcover, $14.95

Quest of Soul - *New Publication!*
In Quest of Soul, Master Ni addresses many subjects relevant to understanding one's own soul, such as the religious concept of saving the soul, how to improve the quality of the personal soul, the high spiritual achievement of free soul, what happens spiritually at death and the universal soul. He guides the reader into deeper knowledge of oneself and inspires each individual to move forward to increase both one's own personal happiness and spiritual level. 152 pages. Stock No. BQUES Softcover, $11.95

Nurture Your Spirits - *New Publication!*
With truthful spiritual knowledge, you have better life attitudes that are more supportive to your existence. With truthful spiritual knowledge, nobody can cause you spiritual confusion. Where can you find such advantage? It would take a lifetime of development in a correct school, but such a school is not available. However, in this book, Master Ni breaks some spiritual prohibitions and presents the spiritual truth he has studied and proven. This truth may help you develop and nurture your own spirits which are the truthful internal foundation of your life being. Taoism is educational; its purpose is not to group people to build social strength but to help each individual build one's own spiritual strength. 176 pages. Stock No. BNURT Softcover, $12.95

Internal Growth Through Tao - *New Publication!*
Material goods can be passed from one person to another, but growth and awareness cannot be given in the same way. Spiritual development is related to one's own internal and external beingness. Through books, discussion or classes, wise people are able to use others' experiences to kindle their own inner light to help their own growth and live a life of no separation from their own spiritual nature. In this book, Master Ni teaches the more subtle, much deeper sphere of the reality of life that is above the shallow sphere of external achievement. He also shows the confusion caused by some spiritual teachings and guides you in the direction of developing spiritually by growing internally. 208 pages. Stock No. BINTE Softcover, $13.95

Power of Natural Healing - *New Publication!*
Master Ni discusses the natural capability of self-healing in this book, which is healing physical trouble untreated by medication or external measure. He offers information and practices which can assist any treatment method currently being used by someone seeking health. He goes deeper to discuss methods of Taoist cultivation which promote a healthy life, including Taoist spiritual achievement, which brings about health and longevity. This book is not only suitable for a person seeking to improve one's health condition. Those who wish to live long and happy, and to understand more about living a natural healthy lifestyle, may be supported by the practice of Taoist energy cultivation. 230 pages. Stock No. BHEAL Softcover, $14.95

Essence of Universal Spirituality
In this volume, as an open-minded learner and achieved teacher of universal spirituality, Master Ni examines and discusses all levels and topics of religious and spiritual teaching to help you develop your own correct knowledge of the essence existing above the differences in religious practice. He reviews religious teachings with hope to benefit modern people. This book is to help readers to come to understand the ultimate truth and enjoy the

achievement of all religions without becoming confused by them. 304 pages. Stock No. BESSE Softcover, $19.95

Guide to Inner Light
Modern life is controlled by city environments, cultural customs, religious teachings and politics that can all divert our attention away from our natural life being. As a result, we lose the perspective of viewing ourselves as natural completeness. This book reveals the development of ancient Taoist adepts. Drawing inspiration from their experience, modern people looking for the true source and meaning of life can find great teachings to direct and benefit them. The invaluable ancient Taoist development can teach us to reach the attainable spiritual truth and point the way to the Inner Light. Master Ni uses the ancient high accomplishments to make this book a useful resource. 192 pages. Stock No. BGUID. Softcover, $12.95

Stepping Stones for Spiritual Success
In Asia, the custom of foot binding was followed for close to a thousand years. In the West, people did not practice foot binding, but they bound their thoughts for a much longer period, some 1,500 to 1,700 years. Their mind and thinking became unnatural. Being unnatural expresses a state of confusion where people do not know what is right. Once they become natural again, they become clear and progress is great. Master Ni invites his readers to unbind their minds; in this volume, he has taken the best of the traditional teachings and put them into contemporary language to make them more relevant to our time, culture and lives. 160 pages. Stock No. BSTEP. Softcover, $12.95.

The Complete Works of Lao Tzu
Lao Tzu's Tao Teh Ching is one of the most widely translated and cherished works of literature in the world. It presents the core of Taoist philosophy. Lao Tzu's timeless wisdom provides a bridge to the subtle spiritual truth and practical guidelines for harmonious and peaceful living. Master Ni has included what is believed to be the only English translation of the Hua Hu Ching, a later work of Lao Tzu which has been lost to the general public for a thousand years. 212 pages. Stock No. BCOMP. Softcover, $12.95

Order The Complete Works of Lao Tzu and the companion Tao Teh Ching Cassette Tapes for only $23.00. Stock No. ABTAO.

The Book of Changes and the Unchanging Truth
The first edition of this book was widely appreciated by its readers, who drew great spiritual benefit from it. They found the principles of the I Ching to be clearly explained and useful to their lives, especially the helpful commentaries. The legendary classic I Ching is recognized as mankind's first written book of wisdom. Leaders and sages throughout history

have consulted it as a trusted advisor which reveals the appropriate action to be taken in any of life's circumstances. This volume also includes over 200 pages of background material on Taoist principles of natural energy cycles, instruction and commentaries. New, revised second edition, 669 pages. Stock No. BBOOK. Hardcover, $35.50

The Story of Two Kingdoms

This volume is the metaphoric tale of the conflict between the Kingdoms of Light and Darkness. Through this unique story, Master Ni transmits the esoteric teachings of Taoism which have been carefully guarded secrets for over 5,000 years. This book is for those who are serious in their search and have devoted their lives to achieving high spiritual goals. 122 pages. Stock No. BSTOR. Hardcover, $14.50

The Way of Integral Life

This book can help build a bridge for those wishing to connect spiritual and intellectual development. It is most helpful for modern educated people. It includes practical and applicable suggestions for daily life, philosophical thought, esoteric insight and guidelines for those aspiring to give help and service to the world. This book helps you learn the wisdom of the ancient sages' achievement to assist the growth of your own wisdom and integrate it as your own new light and principles for balanced, reasonable living in worldly life. 320 pages. Softcover, $14.00, Stock No. BWAYS. Hardcover, $20.00, Stock No. BWAYH

Enlightenment: Mother of Spiritual Independence

The inspiring story and teachings of Master Hui Neng, the father of Zen Buddhism and Sixth Patriarch of the Buddhist tradition, highlight this volume. Hui Neng was a person of ordinary birth, intellectually unsophisticated, who achieved himself to become a spiritual leader. Master Ni includes enlivening commentaries and explanations of the principles outlined by this spiritual revolutionary. Having received the same training as all Zen Masters as one aspect of his training and spiritual achievement, Master Ni offers this teaching so that his readers may be guided in their process of spiritual development. 264 pages. Softcover, $12.50, Stock No. BENLS. Hardcover, $22.00, Stock No. BENLH

Attaining Unlimited Life

The thought-provoking teachings of Chuang Tzu are presented in this volume. He was perhaps the greatest philosopher and master of Taoism and he laid the foundation for the Taoist school of thought. Without his work, people of later generations would hardly recognize the value of Lao Tzu's teaching in practical, everyday life. He touches the organic nature of human life more deeply and directly than that of other great teachers. This volume also includes questions by students and answers by Master Ni. 467 pages. Softcover, $18.00, Stock No. BATTS; Hardcover, $25.00, Stock No. BATTH

Special Discount: Order the three classics Way of Integral Life, Enlightenment: Mother of Spiritual Independence *and* Attaining Unlimited Light *in the hardbound editions, Stock No.* BHARD *for $60.00.*

The Gentle Path of Spiritual Progress
This book offers a glimpse into the dialogues of a Taoist master and his students. In a relaxed, open manner, Master Ni, Hua-Ching explains to his students the fundamental practices that are the keys to experiencing enlightenment in everyday life. Many of the traditional secrets of Taoist training are revealed. His students also ask a surprising range of questions, and Master Ni's answers touch on contemporary psychology, finances, sexual advice, how to use the I Ching as well as the telling of some fascinating Taoist legends. Softcover, $12.95, Stock No. BGENT

Spiritual Messages from a Buffalo Rider, A Man of Tao
This is another important collection of Master Ni's service in his worldly trip, originally published as one half of The Gentle Path. He had the opportunity to meet people and answer their questions to help them gain the spiritual awareness that we live at the command of our animal nature. Our buffalo nature rides on us, whereas an achieved person rides the buffalo. In this book, Master Ni gives much helpful knowledge to those who are interested in improving their lives and deepening their cultivation so they too can develop beyond their mundane beings. Softcover, $12.95, Stock No. BSPIR

8,000 Years of Wisdom, Volume I and II
This two volume set contains a wealth of practical, down-to-earth advice given by Master Ni to his students over a five year period, 1979 to 1983. Drawing on his training in Traditional Chinese Medicine, Herbology, Acupuncture and other Taoist arts, Master Ni gives candid answers to students' questions on many topics ranging from dietary guidance to sex and pregnancy, meditation techniques and natural cures for common illnesses. Volume I includes dietary guidance; 236 pages; Stock No. BWIS1 Volume II includes sex and pregnancy guidance; 241 pages; Stock No. BWIS2. Softcover, Each Volume $12.50

Special discount: Both Books I and II of 8,000 Years of Wisdom, Stock No. BWIS3, for $22.00.

The Uncharted Voyage Towards the Subtle Light
Spiritual life in the world today has become a confusing mixture of dying traditions and radical novelties. People who earnestly and sincerely seek something more than just a way to fit into the complexities of a modern structure that does not support true self-development often find themselves spiritually struggling. This book provides a profound understanding and insight into the underlying heart of all paths of spiritual growth, the subtle origin and the eternal truth of one universal life. 424 pages. Stock No. BUNCH. Softcover, $14.50

The Heavenly Way
A translation of the classic Tai Shan Kan Yin Pien (Straighten Your Way) and Yin Chia Wen (The Silent Way of Blessing). The treaties in this booklet are the main guidance for a mature and healthy life. The purpose of this booklet is to promote the recognition of truth, because only truth can teach the perpetual Heavenly Way by which one reconnects oneself with the divine nature. 41 pages. Stock No. BHEAV. Softcover, $2.50

Special Discount: Order the Heavenly Way in a set of 10 - great for gifts or giveaways. (One shipping item). BHIV10 $17.50.

Footsteps of the Mystical Child
This book poses and answers such questions as: What is a soul? What is wisdom? What is spiritual evolution? The answers to these and many other questions enable readers to open themselves to new realms of understanding and personal growth. There are also many true examples about people's internal and external struggles on the path of self-development and spiritual evolution. 166 pages. Stock No. BFOOT. Softcover, $9.50

Workbook for Spiritual Development
This book offers a practical, down-to-earth, hands-on approach for those who are devoted to the path of spiritual achievement. The reader will find diagrams showing fundamental hand positions to increase and channel one's spiritual energy, postures for sitting, standing and sleeping cultivation as well as postures for many Taoist invocations. The material in this workbook is drawn from the traditional teachings of Taoism and summarizes thousands of years of little known practices for spiritual development. An entire section is devoted to ancient invocations, another on natural celibacy and another on postures. In addition, Master Ni explains the basic attitudes and understandings that are the foundation for Taoist practices. 224 pages. Stock No. BWORK. Softcover, $12.95

Poster of Master Lu
Color poster of Master Lu, Tung Ping (shown on cover of workbook), for use with the workbook or in one's shrine. 16" x 22"; Stock No. PMLTP. $10.95

Order the Workbook for Spiritual Development *and the companion* Poster of Master Lu *for $18.95.* Stock No. BPWOR.

The Taoist Inner View of the Universe
This presentation of Taoist metaphysics provides guidance for one's own personal life transformation. Master Ni has given all the opportunity to know the vast achievement of the ancient unspoiled mind and its transpiercing vision. This book offers a glimpse of the inner

world and immortal realm known to achieved Taoists and makes it understandable for students aspiring to a more complete life. 218 pages. Stock No. BTAOI. Softcover, $14.95

Tao, the Subtle Universal Law
Most people are unaware that their thoughts and behavior evoke responses from the invisible net of universal energy. The real meaning of Taoist self-discipline is to harmonize with universal law. To lead a good stable life is to be aware of the actual conjoining of the universal subtle law with every moment of our lives. This book presents the wisdom and practical methods that the ancient Chinese have successfully used for centuries to accomplish this. 165 pages. Stock No. TAOS. Softcover, $7.50

MATERIALS ON TAOIST HEALTH, ARTS AND SCIENCES

BOOKS

The Tao of Nutrition by Maoshing Ni, Ph.D., with Cathy McNease, B.S., M.H. - Working from ancient Chinese medical classics and contemporary research, Dr. Maoshing Ni and Cathy McNease have compiled an indispensable guide to natural healing. This exceptional book shows the reader how to take control of one's health through one's eating habits. This volume contains 3 major sections: the first section deals with theories of Chinese nutrition and philosophy; the second describes over 100 common foods in detail, listing their energetic properties, therapeutic actions and individual remedies. The third section lists nutritional remedies for many common ailments. This book presents both a healing system and a disease prevention system which is flexible in adapting to every individual's needs. 214 pages. Stock No. BNUTR. Softcover, $14.50

Chinese Vegetarian Delights by Lily Chuang
An extraordinary collection of recipes based on principles of traditional Chinese nutrition. Many recipes are therapeutically prepared with herbs. Diet has long been recognized as a key factor in health and longevity. For those who require restricted diets and those who choose an optimal diet, this cookbook is a rare treasure. Meat, sugar, diary products and fried foods are excluded. Produce, grains, tofu, eggs and seaweeds are imaginatively prepared. 104 pages. Stock No. BCHIV. Softcover, $7.50

Chinese Herbology Made Easy - by Maoshing Ni, Ph.D.
This text provides an overview of Oriental medical theory, in-depth descriptions of each herb category, with over 300 black and white photographs, extensive tables of individual herbs for easy reference, and an index of pharmaceutical and Pin-Yin names. The distillation of overwhelming material into essential elements enables one to focus efficiently and develop a clear understanding of Chinese herbology. This book is especially helpful for those studying for their California Acupuncture License. 202 pages. Stock No. BCHIH. Softcover, 14.50

Crane Style Chi Gong Book - By Daoshing Ni, Ph.D.
Chi Gong is a set of meditative exercises that was developed several thousand years ago by Taoists in China. It is now practiced for healing purposes, combining breathing techniques, body movements and mental imagery to guide the smooth flow of energy throughout the body. This book gives a more detailed account and study of Chi Gong than the videotape alone. It may be used with or without the videotape. Includes complete instructions and information on using Chi Gong exercise as a medical therapy. 55 pages. Stock No. BCRAN. Spiral bound $10.50

VIDEO TAPES

Physical Movement for Spiritual Learning: Dao-In Physical Art for a Long and Happy Life (VHS) - by Master Ni. Dao-In is a series of typical Taoist movements which are traditionally used for physical energy conducting. These exercises were passed down from the ancient achieved Taoists and immortals. The ancients discovered that Dao-In exercises not only solved problems of stagnant energy, but also increased their health and lengthened their years. The exercises are also used as practical support for cultivation and the higher achievements of spiritual immortality. Master Ni, Hua-Ching, heir to the tradition of the achieved masters, is the first one who releases this important Taoist practice to the modern world in this 1 hour videotape. Stock No. VDAOI VHS $59.95

T'ai Chi Chuan: An Appreciation (VHS) - by Master Ni - Different styles of T'ai Chi Ch'uan as Movement have different purposes and accomplish different results. In this long awaited videotape, Master Ni, Hua-Ching presents three styles of T'ai Chi Movement handed down to him through generations of highly developed masters. They are the "Gentle Path," "Sky Journey," and "Infinite Expansion" styles of T'ai Chi Movement. The three styles are presented uninterrupted in this unique videotape and are set to music for observation and appreciation. Stock No. VAPPR. VHS 30 minutes $49.95

Crane Style Chi Gong (VHS) - by Dr. Daoshing Ni, Ph.D.
Chi Gong is a set of meditative exercises developed several thousand years ago by ancient Taoists in China. It is now practiced for healing stubborn chronic diseases, strengthening the body to prevent disease and as a tool for further spiritual enlightenment. It combines breathing techniques, simple body movements, and mental imagery to guide the smooth flow of energy throughout the body. Chi gong is easy to learn for all ages. Correct and persistent practice will increase one's energy, relieve stress or tension, improve concentration and clarity, release emotional stress and restore general well-being. 2 hours Stock No. VCRAN. $65.95

Eight Treasures (VHS) - By Maoshing Ni, Ph.D.
These exercises help open blocks in a person's energy flow and strengthen one's vitality. It is a complete exercise combining physical stretching and toning and energy conducting movements coordinated with breathing. The Eight Treasures are an exercise unique to the Ni family. Patterned from nature, its 32 movements are an excellent foundation for Tai Chi Chuan or martial arts. 1 hour, 45 minutes. Stock No. VEIGH. $49.95

Tai Chi Chuan I & II (VHS) - By Maoshing Ni, Ph.D.
This exercise integrates the flow of physical movement with that of integral energy in the Taoist style of "Harmony," similar to the long form of Yang-style Tai Chi Chuan. Tai Chi has been practiced for thousands of years to help both physical longevity and spiritual cultivation. 1 hour each. Each Video Tape $49.95. Order both for $90.00. Stock Nos: Part I, VTAI1; Part II, VTAI2; Set of two, VTAI3.

AUDIO CASSETTES

Invocations: Health and Longevity and Healing a Broken Heart - By Maoshing Ni, Ph.D. *Updated with additional material!* This audio cassette guides the listener through a series of ancient invocations to channel and conduct one's own healing energy and vital force. "Thinking is louder than thunder." The mystical power by which all miracles are brought about is your sincere practice of this principle. 30 minutes. Stock No. AINVO. $8.95

Chi Gong for Stress Release - By Maoshing Ni, Ph.D.
This audio cassette guides you through simple, ancient breathing exercises that enable you to release day-to-day stress and tension that are such a common cause of illness today. 30 minutes. Stock No. ACHIS. $8.95

Chi Gong for Pain Management - By Maoshing Ni, Ph.D.
Using easy visualization and deep-breathing techniques that have been developed over thousands of years, this audio cassette offers methods for overcoming pain by invigorating your energy flow and unblocking obstructions that cause pain. 30 minutes. Stock No. ACHIP. $8.95

Tao Teh Ching Cassette Tapes
This classic work of Lao Tzu has been recorded in this two-cassette set that is a companion to the book translated by Master Ni. Professionally recorded and read by Robert Rudelson. 120 minutes. Stock No. ATAOT. $15.95

Order Master Ni's book, The Complete Works of Lao Tzu, and Tao Teh Ching Cassette Tapes for only $25.00. Stock No. ABTAO.

This list of Master Ni's books in English is ordered by date of publication for those readers who wish to follow the sequence of his Western teaching material in their learning of Tao.

1979:   *The Complete Works of Lao Tzu*
        The Taoist Inner View of the Universe
        Tao, the Subtle Universal Law
1983:   *The Book of Changes and the Unchanging Truth*
        8,000 Years of Wisdom, I
        8,000 Years of Wisdom, II
1984:   *Workbook for Spiritual Development*
1985:   *The Uncharted Voyage Towards the Subtle Light*
1986:   *Footsteps of the Mystical Child*
1987:   *The Gentle Path of Spiritual Progress*
        Spiritual Messages from a Buffalo Rider, (originally
                part of *Gentle Path of Spiritual Progress*)
1989:   *The Way of Integral Life*
        Enlightenment: Mother of Spiritual Independence
        Attaining Unlimited Life
        The Story of Two Kingdoms
1990:   *Stepping Stones for Spiritual Success*
        Guide to Inner Light
        Essence of Universal Spirituality
1991:   *Internal Growth through Tao*
        Nurture Your Spirits
        Quest of Soul
        Power of Natural Healing
        *Attune Your Body with Dao-In: Taoist Exercise for a Long and
                Happy Life*
        Eternal Light
        Harmony: The Art of Life
        The Key to Good Fortune: Refining Your Spirit
        Moonlight in the Dark Night

In addition, the forthcoming books will be compiled from his lecturing and teaching service:

Golden Message: The Tao in Your Daily Life (by Daoshing and
        Maoshing Ni, based on the works of Master Ni, Hua-Ching)
Learning Gentle Path T'ai Chi Chuan
Learning Sky Journey T'ai Chi Chuan
Learning Infinite Expansion T'ai Chi Chuan
Learning Cosmic Tour Ba Gua
The Mystical Universal Mother
Taoist Mysticism: The Uniting of God and Human Life
Life and Teachings of Two Immortals, Volume I: Kou Hong
Life and Teachings of Two Immortals, Volume II: Chen Tuan

How To Order

Name:

Address:

City: State: Zip:

Phone - Daytime: Evening:

(We may telephone you if we have questions about your order.)

Qty.	Stock No.	Title/Description	Price Each	Total Price

Total amount for items ordered_____

Sales tax (CA residents only, 8-1/4%)_____

Shipping Charge (See below)_____

Total Amount Enclosed_____

Visa _____ Mastercard _____ Expiration Date _____

Card number:_____

Signature:_____

Shipping: In the US, we use UPS when possible. Please give full street address or nearest crossroads. All packages are insured at no extra charge. If shipping to more than one address, use separate shipping charges. Remember: 1 - 10 copies of Heavenly Way, Tao Teh Ching audio tapes and each book and tape are single items. Posters (up to 5 per tube) are a separate item. Please allow 2 - 4 weeks for US delivery and 6 - 10 weeks for foreign surface mail.

By Mail: Complete this form with payment (US funds only, No Foreign Postal Money Orders, please) and mail to: Union of Tao and Man, 117 Stonehaven Way, Los Angeles, CA 90049

Phone Orders: (213) 472-9970 - You may leave credit card orders anytime on our answering machine. Please speak clearly and remember to leave your full name and daytime phone number. We will call only if we have a question with your order, there is a delay or you specifically ask for phone confirmation.

Inquiries: If you have questions concerning your order, please refer to the date and invoice number on the top center of your invoice to help us locate your order swiftly.

Shipping Charges -
     Domestic Surface: First item $3.25, each additional, add $.50.
     Canada Surface: First item $3.25, each additional, add $1.00.
     Canada Air: First item $4.00, each additional, add $2.00
     Foreign Surface: First Item $3.50, each additional, add $2.00.
     Foreign Air: First item $12.00, each additional, add $7.00.

For the Trade: Wholesale orders may be placed direct to publisher, or with NewLeaf, BookPeople, The Distributors, Inland Books, GreatWay in US or DeepBooks in Europe.

Thank you for your order

Spiritual Study Through the College of Tao

The College of Tao and the Union of Tao and Man were established formally in California in the 1970's. This tradition is a very old spiritual culture of mankind, holding long experience of human spiritual growth. Its central goal is to offer healthy spiritual education to all people of our society. This time tested tradition values the spiritual development of each individual self and passes down its guidance and experience.

Master Ni carries his tradition from its country of origin to the west. He chooses to avoid making the mistake of old-style religions that have rigid establishments which resulted in fossilizing the delicacy of spiritual reality. Rather, he prefers to guide the teachings of his tradition as a school of no boundary rather than a religion with rigidity. Thus, the branches or centers of this Taoist school offer different programs of similar purpose. Each center extends its independent service, but all are unified in adopting Master Ni's work as the foundation of teaching to fulfill the mission of providing spiritual education to all people.

The centers offer their classes, teaching, guidance and practices on building the groundwork for cultivating a spiritually centered and well-balanced life. As a person obtains the correct knowledge with which to properly guide himself or herself, he or she can then become more skillful in handling the experiences of daily life. The assimilation of good guidance in one's practical life brings about different stages of spiritual development.

Any interested individual is welcome to join and learn to grow for oneself. You might like to join the center near where you live, or you yourself may be interested in organizing a center or study group based on the model of existing centers. In that way, we all work together for the spiritual benefit of all people. We do not require any religious type of commitment.

The learning is life. The development is yours. The connection of study may be helpful, useful and serviceable, directly to you.

- -

Mail to: Union of Tao and Man, 117 Stonehaven Way, Los Angeles, CA 90049

____ I wish to be put on the mailing list of the Union of Tao and Man to be notified of classes, educational activities and new publications.

Name:_____

Address:_____

City:_____State:_____Zip:_____

Herbs Used by Ancient Taoist Masters

The pursuit of everlasting youth or immortality throughout human history is an innate human desire. Long ago, Chinese esoteric Taoists went to the high mountains to contemplated nature, strengthen their bodies, empower their minds and develop their spirit. From their studies and cultivation, they gave China alchemy and chemistry, herbology and acupuncture, the I Ching, astrology, martial arts and T'ai Chi Chuan, Chi Gong and many other useful kinds of knowledge.

Most important, they handed down in secrecy methods for attaining longevity and spiritual immortality. There were different levels of approach; one was to use a collection of food herb formulas that were only available to highly achieved Taoist masters. They used these food herbs to increase energy and heighten vitality. This treasured collection of herbal formulas remained within the Ni family for centuries.

Now, through Traditions of Tao, the Ni family makes these foods available for you to use to assist the foundation of your own positive development. It is only with a strong foundation that expected results are produced from diligent cultivation.

As a further benefit, in concert with the Taoist principle of self-sufficiency, Traditions of Tao offers the food herbs along with the Union of Tao and Man's publications in a distribution opportunity for anyone serious about financial independence.

Send to: *Traditions of Tao*
             c/o 117 Stonehaven Way
             Los Angeles, CA 90049

☐ *Please send me a Traditions of Tao brochure.*

☐ *Please send me information on becoming an independent distributor of Traditions of Tao herbal products and publications.*

Name _____

Address _____

City _____*State* _____*Zip* _____

Phone (day) _____*(night)* _____

Yo San University of Traditional Chinese Medicine

"Not just a medical career, but a life-time commitment to raising one's spiritual standard."

Thank you for your support and interest in our publications and services. It is by your patronage that we continue to offer you the practical knowledge and wisdom from this venerable Taoist tradition.

Because of your sustained interest in Taoism, we formed Yo San University of Traditional Chinese Medicine, a non-profit educational institute in January 1989 under the direction of founder Master Ni, Hua-Ching. Yo San University is the continuation of 38 generations of Ni family practitioners who handed down knowledge and wisdom from fathers to sons. Its purpose is to train and graduate practitioners of the highest caliber in Traditional Chinese Medicine, which includes acupuncture, herbology and spiritual development.

We view Traditional Chinese Medicine as the application of spiritual development. Its foundation is the spiritual capability to know life, to know a person's problem and how to cure it. We teach students how to care for themselves and others, and emphasize the integration of traditional knowledge and modern science. We offer a complete Master's degree program approved by the California State Department of Education that provides an excellent education in Traditional Chinese Medicine and meets all requirements for state licensure.

We invite you to inquire into our school about a creative and rewarding career as a holistic physician. Classes are also open to persons interested only in self-enrichment. For more information, please fill out the form below and send it to:

Yo San University,
12304 Santa Monica Blvd. Suite 104,
Los Angeles, CA 90025

☐ Please send me information on the Masters degree program in Traditional Chinese Medicine.

☐ Please send me information on health workshops and seminars.

☐ Please send me information on continuing education for acupuncturists and health professionals.

Name _____

Address_____

City_____State_____Zip_____

Phone(day)_____(night)_____